S.S.O.T.B.M.E.

REVISED

AN ESSAY ON MAGIC

> Mr Dukes, why is it that in this and other writings you insist on personifying complex processes as 'demons' or spirits'. Isn't this just a throw-back to superstitions of the past?

That depends whether you believe the superior brain of homo sapiens was developed to handle tools, or social relationships. If you believe that the most complex processes we have to deal with are our fellow humans, then greater brainpower is available for life's problems when you anthropomorphise them.

> But we *know* that the weather, or my car, is only a mechanical phenomenon. It is a false initial assumption to address it as a god.

One of the first things you learn in interpersonal relationships is how often people behave mechanically. Mechanistic explanations are not distinct from personal ones, they are merely a subset. If, for example, my car fails to start at times when I'm rushed, the irrational question "how does it know I am in a hurry" may lead to a solution faster than the rational statement "it cannot possibly know". The fault will probably turn out to be mechanical, just as human misbehaviour often resolves into "you pressed my buttons". Irrational thinking can often be the faster route to a rational solution.

> You really think science is no more than a dumbing down of magic?

That is not what I argue in this book. I only want to challenge the common idea that magic is a dumbing down of science.

> Science cannot be dumber than magic, because it has been so much more materially successful!

Any media cynic will tell you that dumbing down is the key to material success! No, the point is that, in terms of the faculties used, magical thinking is broader, but maybe not as deep.

You do not like the fact that a society of rational beings rewards dumbness. Instead of fretting, just call it 'Satan's Jewel Crown'. No matter whether you fight it like a preacher, or make a pact with it like a press baron - in either case you are personifying it, relating to it, and that can be magic.

S.S.O.T.B.M.E.

REVISED

an essay on magic

Edited and revised by

Ramsey Dukes

SSOTBME
REVISED

Edited and revised by Ramsey Dukes

Originally published by the Mouse That Spins, England, 1974
Second English edition 1975
First US edition, Grey Turner/Weiser, 1979
First Polish edition, 198?
First German edition, 198?
Second Polish edition, 1992
Revised e-book edition, 2000

This revised edition published on demand 2001 onward
by The Mouse That Spins

ISBN: 0-904311-08-2

Cover Illustration: *The Blasé Bacchante* by Austin Osman Spare

E-books available at occultebooks.com
books@web-orama.com / publisher@el-cheapo.com

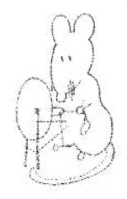 the mouse that spins

CONTENTS

CONTENTS

PREFACE TO THE REVISED 1998 EDITION

Here is a new, revised edition of a book first published by The Mouse That Spins in April 1975 as *'SSOTBME' an essay on magic, its foundations, development and place in modern life*. Since then it has run to two English, one American, two Polish and at least one German edition — and earned many friends along the way.

HISTORICAL BACKGROUND

The book was originally conceived in 1974 as an essay to be included within a longer book. Christopher MacIntosh had proposed a collection of essays on topics such as Tantricism, Zen Buddhism and other exotic religious ideas which had been attracting wider interest in the West since the hippy era — and he thought it would be rather interesting to include a piece on Western Ritual Magic. The required contribution was written, but the book idea was shelved (as it were). That left a nice essay which was worth editing and publishing in its own right.

The publishing house was called 'The Mouse That Spins' because Companies' House would not permit my use of 'The Imperial Publishing House Of Great Britain' — a name which I considered rather cool and revolutionary at the time.

It is less easy to explain why the book was originally published anonymously. So I won't.

Ramsey Dukes was asked to revise the text for this edition, on the assumption that he wrote the essay — however his style was more verbose than the original (maybe an effect of the corrupting influence of word processors since 1974) so his main additions have been ghettoised into appended chapters in smaller print in order to preserve the integrity of the original.

The essay was written at a time when there was a big gulf between public ideas of the occult — typified perhaps by the film The Exorcist — and what magical groups were actually doing. All that was intended was to cast a fresh eye across this gulf and see if it bounced. Nice metaphor.

It was Gerald Suster who made the perceptive observation that SSOTBME was "the book that put the magic back into magic". At that time serious magic in Britain was heavily under the influence of writers like Dion Fortune and WE Butler, writers with a strongly psychological approach. Their contribution was crucial for keeping the magical traditions alive during materialistic times, but the downside was that magic came to be practiced more as a sophisticated form of psychotherapy than as a way of living one's life.

What Gerald saw was that the simple ideas expressed in SSOTBME actually revived the whole possibility of magical interaction with everyday reality. Thanks to his insight, SSOTBME was to play a seminal role in the early days of the Chaos Magic movement. Others have claimed SSOTBME as a key influence on the New Age movement of the 80s.

THE NEED TO REPUBLISH

I heard Richard Dawkins on BBC television last year expressing anxiety at the rising interest in paranormal pseudo-science, and his theme was taken up by an anxious panel on BBC Radio's Moral Maze. It sounded like a throw-back to the 50s when people used to believe that magic was a sort of primi-tive forerunner to modern science. Believe that, then any resurgence of interest in magical ideas must indeed seem as a reversal of civilisation.

I could live with mankind's final slide into crazed degeneracy, what really scared me was this evidence that there were people — otherwise quite intel-ligent — who had apparently not yet read SSOTBME. A new edition was urgently needed in response to this cry for help.

THE NEED TO REVISE

As SSOTBME has been long out of print, all that is really needed is a reprint. However, twenty five years have elapsed and the world has evolved. Dukes could rewrite the whole thing and create a new book, but there is a certain interest in returning to source and preserving the original text.

So this edition is a compromise. Changes have been made to the text, but the main updating is appended in additional sections. The changes include editorial tidying (with less use of brackets (and footnotes)) and rewording of some insupportable sentences. The additional sections are a new introduction and appendices to most chapters.

The biggest change is that the content of the old Chapter 9 has been brought forward to Chapter 3A to help illustrate the ebb and flow of Magical thinking and provide further illustration of a Magical as opposed to a Scientific theory.

INTRODUCTION

Imagine this situation.

A well-established manufacturer — let us say a renowned Northampton shoe maker — is proud of its tradition and reputation, but aware of rising costs and flagging sales: it consults a marketing specialist and spends a great deal of money for advice which can be summarised as follows.

"Your image is far too staid and respectable. You should sharpen it up to appeal to a new, younger customer base. Italicise your logo, use brighter colours, employ more young sales staff and add humour and zip to your promotions."

If challenged to justify such trendy mumbo jumbo, the consultant would probably get a bit huffy and insist that his company works on sound scientific principles. Pages of statistics, analysis and market research would be produced to justify this claim.

But what if the manufacturer had instead consulted a traditional magician? He would have been advised as follows. "You need to invoke the help of Mercury, because he is the god of commerce. He is also the god of youth, swiftness, communication, trickery and his magical images use yellow and bright colours. So add a bit of yellow or bright colour to your logo, italicise it to show swiftness, employ more young people, think more youthfully and put some humour and zip into your promotions. Most appropriate of all for a god who rules communications — you should create a trendy web site."

The justification may be quite different, yet the actions prescribed are almost identical. So what is going on?

The book argues that, to really understand magic and its place in our society, it is more helpful to begin by considering it as a different way of thinking rather than as a distinct type of activity.

If you dismiss, say, Jungian psychological approaches to magic because you insist that 'real' magic is all about robes, incense, barbaric conjurations and ritual sacrifice, then you are doing no better than someone who insists that scientists are not 'real' unless they have hair like Einstein, thick spectacles and white lab coats; or that 'real' artists must be penniless; or that 'true' religious believers must be dogmatic fundamentalists.

This book attempts not only to explain the essence of magic, but also why those marketing specialists feel compelled to justify their advice as 'scientifically sound', when it is pretty obvious that they and many others are actually practicing magic.

I would like this book to reach out to people who are naturally drawn to magical thinking, but have been persuaded by our culture that there is no such thing and, anyway, it is 'wrong'.

It would also be nice if it reaches other people who reject magical thinking, provided that it explains to them the nature of that rejected path, and it thereby saves them from falling into magic unawares.

We might all think more clearly if we knew what we were doing.

He came from an engineering background but was now passionate about the occult. So I showed him my diagram of the relationship between Magic, Art, Religion and Science.

"Sorry" he exclaimed "I've no time for putting things into neat little boxes!"

I showed him a compass-rose... but he saw neat little boxes. A good example of the difference between a Magical and a Scientific perspective. It also showed how some feel bound to abandon analysis in their flight from Science.

Maybe if we thought in terms of directions rather than boxes we could attain a different sort of clarity? One which assisted human communication without constraining it?

CHAPTER ONE
The basic definition of Magic

Magic is a technique by which the human mind attempts to operate upon its world. As such it is similar to Art, Religion and Science, but note that the term 'its world' is meant to embrace not only the physical universe but also all phenomena, objective or subjective, which do not respond to direct control. So it is, up to a point, true to say that the above mentioned systems in varying measure are also used to operate upon the human itself.

In what way then does Magic differ from Art, Religion or Science? Obvious practical differences in observed technique suggest themselves, and yet do not lead us to fundamental distinction when pursued. We can also attempt to distinguish by saying, for example, that Magic uses 'mysterious forces' where Science uses 'known laws'. But surely that would mean that we would often have to use the word 'Magic' to discuss future Scientific projects? Although the forces used by Magicians do not necessarily seem mysterious to the users, there is a school of thought which would defend the idea that Magic is the Science of as-yet-undiscovered forces. It is an idea which appeals to what we might (without intended malice) call the 'pseudo scientists' eg dowsers and anthroposophists. But surely the more fundamental distinction lies not in the outward methods, but in the thinking which underlies them?

A simple act, such as the lighting of a fire under difficult conditions, could be performed in the same skilful way, but according to quite different mental processes. In two of those ways, the Magical and the Scientific, the outcome might appear to hold more practical importance and yet the reasoning is different. The Scientific thinker would take trouble to choose dry kindling because, for example, he knows that the latent heat of evaporation of absorbed water would hinder ignition; but the Magical thinker would make the same decision because he knows that the elements Fire and Water are antipathetic. In the case of the fire ignited as a Religious act, or an Artistic act, the motivation appears less practical and more a result of inner prompting. Although the Religious thinker is more inclined to choose dry wood because tradition demands it, thus disguising logic, he is also likely to make full use of the Scientist's reasoning as long as it is recognised as a God-given ability. On the other hand, the Artistic thinker would choose dry wood because it 'feels right', a reasoning closer to that of the Magician.

In distinguishing the modes of thought, we come to a similar conclusion to that of C. G. Jung: that thought is compounded of four elements which I call intuition, observation, logic and feeling.

Two of those are ways in which impressions reach us. In observation they come via the senses, in intuition, they do not; instead they come via memory or as a sudden 'inspiration' — this is not to say that intuition might not be triggered by the senses.

The other two are methods by which the impressions are linked, or manipulated. Logic is well enough understood, but feeling is less easy to describe because it is a way of associating ideas using the brain's pattern-recognition faculties rather than conscious logic. As such it is perhaps best understood inductively by considering various examples in the course of this essay — this inductive learning itself indicates something of the nature of feeling.

The biggest difficulty is that other people would use the word 'intuition' to describe much of what I call feeling, and use the word 'feeling' to describe emotional responses. My use of 'feeling' is expanded in Chapter 1A, but I will also point out that Fernandez Armasto in his book 'Truth' describes four traditional standards for measuring truth - thinking, sensation, feeling and authority. I realise now that the intuitive basis of Religious thought very often does come as dictation from some outer authority (as in my firelighting example where "tradition demands it"). The role of intuition is then twofold - the obvious one of delivering "the word of God" to certain individuals, and the secondary one of giving listeners an intuitive recognition of which particular individuals (among many conflicting voices) are indeed speaking with authority.

Any practical method of thinking demands at least two of these four elements, one to serve as an input of impressions and the other to process them. Artistic thought uses feeling and intuition, Religious thought uses intuition and logic, Scientific thought uses logic and observation, and Magical thought uses observation and feeling.

This definition of the terms Magical, Artistic, Religious and Scientific is due to Lemuel Johnstone, as are the rest of the arguments and examples of this essay. Although I am happy that they largely reflect the usual meanings of these words, it is possible that the reader will remain unconvinced, and so the initial capitals will be retained throughout this essay as a reminder that all argument will be based on these definitions. In general, however, the terminology of this essay will not be strictly defined.

The definitions may be summarised in the following diagram.

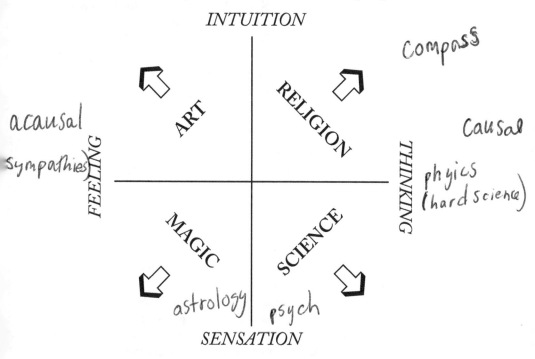

The immediate problem with such a diagram is that the Scientific (in my sense) bias in our culture encourages us to see it as a sort of clock face onto which we can 'place' different disciplines. For example: in the Science sector, more empirical research into, say, psychology and sociology would lie far down between 5 and 6 o'clock whereas purer sciences would lie nearer to 3. Similarly in the Magic sector, astrology and 'pseudo sciences' would lie between 6 and 7 o'clock, divination and ritual magic between 7 and 8 o'clock, and magic systems such as that of Austin Spare nearer to 9 o'clock. Spontaneous religion and art lie close to 12 o'clock, the more academic dogma or political systems lie between 2 and 3 o'clock, and the art of appreciating art lies between 9 and 10 o'clock.

This sort of attribution can, however, be most misleading because the diagram is actually meant to be more of a direction indicator — like the compass North/South/East/West in the corner of a map. In this case the placing of specific disciplines depends upon where you are standing. A more strictly 'Scientific' bias would shift the above placings so that economics and psychology fell into the 'mumbo jumbo' Magic sector, whilst mathematics would fall with philosophy into the Religious sector. A more extreme 'Religious' bias would lump a lot of Art and Science subjects in the Magic sector as 'the Devil's work'. A more 'Artistic' bias would consider astrology and cabalistic philosophy, for example, to be "all too frightfully Scientific, my dear."

The first misunderstanding which must be dealt with is the impression that the above definition in some way belittles the subjects with which it deals. The occultist might accept the Artistic, Religious and Scientific placings, and yet object that it is preposterous to 'lump together' such diverse subjects as astrology, spiritualism and ritual magic as being 'just observation plus feeling'. It must be realised that the mixtures and interactions of thoughts are so involved that the four words 'intuition', 'logic', 'observation' and 'feeling' are also better seen as *directions* than ingredients. So to put both astrology and ritual magic in one quadrant relative to myself does no more to equate them than does the sentence "Bristol and the Scilly Isles are both South West of Cheltenham" mean that Bristol and the Scilly Isles are in any other way the same.

The involved nature of thinking leads to the second objection: surely I don't believe that Scientists never use intuition, and Artists don't observe? This is of course blatantly untrue: in any real life situation we will find all four thought processes apparently inextricably mixed. Again, the answer lies partly in remembering that we are talking of directions and not ingredients — so the question is not so much "what faculties does a scientist use?" but rather "however the

4

discovery was made, which way is the scientist facing? ie how is the discovery justified or defended?"

So you can determine the basis of a particular action by verbally attacking the perpetrators and asking them to defend their action. However inspirational a Scientific discovery, it will be written up and placed before the public judgement as an exercise in reason and observation. Although a painting can be a triumph of acute observation, it is unlikely that the artist will defend it upon such 'photographic' grounds.

The way in which the basic thought can be detected will become clearer later when more examples are considered in detail. So I will end this section with three illustrations of the difference between Magical and Scientific thought, with the particular intention of illustrating further what is meant by 'feeling'.

The first example is very primitive. Imagine two simple people who have both made the same observation, namely that green apples, green plums and old meat which had green mould on it all tended to make people sick when eaten, and that the sick peoples' faces took on a greeny hue. One of the two tackles this observation logically, and sets out, for example, with experiments to locate the green substance in these different foods which makes you sick and subsequently tinges the face. The other uses feeling: he repeats a few experiments and deduces that greenness 'goes with' sickness. The first is thinking Scientifically and the second Magically. Here we can see how Magic is at an advantage in a primitive situation: whilst the first thinker is still testing erroneous theories, the second has already deduced a fairly powerful one: he can proceed to make his enemies ill by serving green food in a room decorated a sickly green.

Because we know much more about Science nowadays, it is natural to criticise my conclusion by pointing out that the Scientist will eventually find out very much more, and that the Magician's rapid conclusion is anyway 'false' because there are so many exceptions to that rule. But this criticism is based on a lack of experience as to how the Magical way of thought might refine and improve its conclusions to the same extent that the Scientific can. For a start, the Magician would soon identify distinct types of greenness: there is the greenness of decay, the greenness of immaturity and so on.

The second example is set in a more familiar situation, but is equally elementary. If you notice that the traffic lights are always red when you are in a desperate hurry, and you dismiss your observation on logical grounds, then you are thinking Scientifically. If instead you accept your observation and try next time to banish the feeling of desperation from your mind in order to avoid red lights, then you are thinking Magically.

This statement is of course unfair: a truly Scientific thinker would give observation and logic equal weight at first. He would, therefore, continue by trying in future to collect statistical evidence that a certain degree of despair went with a certain percentage of red lights; but he would have to abandon the search when he found that this Scientific interest merely served to banish his panic. Finding that the desperate, panicky feeling was too elusively subjective, he would deduce that the apparent excess of red lights was possibly also a subjective illusion, and only then would the inquiry cease.

However, the example is correct insofar as it illustrates a present day degeneration of Scientific thought: as a way of thought, Science has become so familiar that it is dogmatic and liable to take short cuts, and therefore we do find observations being dismissed out of hand in the course of otherwise 'Scientific' thinking.

But what of our Magician? Surely he too will find that the elusive panic vanishes when he takes a Magical interest in it? Precisely, and thus he will conclude that his Magic has 'worked'. There is no practical way to refute this conclusion. One can only resort to abstract wrangles as to whether there was ever a surfeit of red lights in the past.

The third example is a less elementary one. It is intended to show how in the ultimate resort we will uncover the two elements of thinking as described in the definition, even though the other elements are used along the way. As an example of the Scientific thinker, I will take an applied mathematician deducing a formula for the time of flight of a projectile, and for the Magical thought, consider the setting up of a temple to invoke Venus.

The Scientist starts from basic known facts about the elements of his problem and proceeds to cover sheets of paper with a series of logical calculations until the desired formula is attained. The Magician starts from basic known facts about the entity to be invoked

6

and proceeds to decorate a room with all the apparatus, colours, sounds and smells which 'go with' that entity until he is satisfied that the atmosphere 'feels right'. The example stops at this point — the actual invocation to follow could be considered equivalent to the actual use of the projectile formula.

But let us imagine that each has made a mistake in his working. The Scientist sits back in relief, then exclaims: "Hang on, that doesn't seem right. Why hasn't gravitational constant 'g' come into my result?" A mathematician expects to find 'g' in such a formula, so notice that the immediate objection is one of feeling — it doesn't 'seem right'. But of course the objection will not be accepted by him on those grounds. Instead, he will carefully rework the logic of his calculations until the correct answer is achieved. The Magician stands back from his handiwork with relief, then says: "Hang on, I've only got six candles on the altar. That's wrong." Now his objection is a logical one: six is not the number of Venus in the Cabalistic system, but seven is. However, that is insufficient justification for chucking in another candle. The Magician will savour the atmosphere created in his Venusian Temple, and if it seems impossible to add a seventh candle without spoiling the balance and harmony of what he has already done, then he will not do so.

Whereas the Scientist's objection of feeling was resolved by the use of logic, the Magician's objection of logic was resolved by the use of feeling. In each case, it was the ultimate resort which betrayed the true nature.

Readers who have read Crowley might wonder how this fourfold direction scheme stands in relation to his definition of what he called 'Magick', ie the Art and Science of causing change in conformity to Will. He was in a sense placing himself at the centre and using the word Magick to embrace the whole process of willed action. He adds that, of all the methods of Magick, only a certain proportion of them are what would traditionally be described as 'magical'.

Crowley was advocating a bringing together of all techniques, scientific and artistic, under the term 'Magick' ("the Aim of Religion, the Method of Science" to quote his phrase). If I wanted to proselytise, a similar line could be taken. However, I am merely trying here to describe traditional 'magical' techniques.

CHAPTER 1A
Making sense of 'feeling' and 'direction'

As mentioned in Chapter One, the problem with my use of words is that a lot of what I describe as 'feeling' other people would call 'intuition'.

On reflection — the sort of thing one gets round to after 30 years — I would describe the process which makes instant non-causal connections as 'pattern recognition' instead of 'feeling'. But I have retained the word feeling in the rest of the text because people do tend to use that word loosely in order to distinguish the process from logical analysis.

Consider the lone woman opening the door to a slightly scruffy stranger who claims to be from the Water Board. She senses something is wrong and has what she describes as 'a bad feeling' about the man and she can respond in several ways. One is to shut the door in his face and ring the police. Another is to argue with herself that she should not be such a silly, prejudiced woman and then let him in without further question.

My point is that her 'bad feeling' is an immediate sense that the situation — the man, her alone, the request to enter the house — is a pattern which 'goes with' danger. My argument is that this process deserves more respect than it sometimes gets.

In the second behaviour option, the lady calls this process 'prejudice' and over-rules it. Because we are trained to value reason more highly than feeling, reason tends to step in and analyse these feeling judgements — eg "dear, me. Why am I feeling insecure just because the man's shoes are a bit tatty and he looks a bit scruffy? I am becoming as middle class and prejudiced as my Mum!" Reason can nearly always analyse a number of components of any pattern and often is used to dismiss them — eg "scruffy shoes could simply mean poverty, dirty hands could simply mean that he has been turning off a stop-cock in the street, a shifty look could simply mean he is awkward about asking a lone woman to let him into the house" and so on, until the initial sense of danger begins to look like unthinking prejudice.

My argument is that this pattern-recognition process is not so stupid. I believe we have it because it has as much survival value as logical thought. In cases of immediate danger of very rapid decision making it is actually far more useful than the pedestrian process of logical thought. The reason we value logic so much more highly is largely because civilised society allows fewer such immediate threats than our animal past, and so we have forgotten the value of such 'feeling'.

What I suggest is that the woman's initial 'bad feeling' is telling her that 'something is wrong' and that I believe we should learn to trust such feelings.

Something very likely is wrong — but it simply may not turn out to pose a threat. Trusting feeling is not a question of being swept away by it, it is a question of giving it as much value as reason and knowing how to use it.

The woman's senses have taken in zillions of bits of data as she opens that door, and her feeling has detected something amiss in the overall pattern. If, instead of dismissing feeling or panicking, she respects it, she will proceed with caution. She could ask to see his identification documents; she could ask him to remain outside while she phones the Water Board to confirm that an inspector of his description is in the vicinity; she could ask him to return later or whatever. If she feels something is wrong, I suspect that something is wrong; but it could turn out to be something which poses no immediate threat to her — for example, the man might be wracked with bitter divorce proceedings and so neglecting his appearance while doing his best to continue his job to provide income for his family. She has indeed sensed that something is wrong, but it is not 'what we might think'.

I have made much of this example because I want to suggest that our brains have evolved a non-logical data processing facility which is, in its own way, every bit as useful and sophisticated as reason but which we tend to play down or analyse away because its causal connections seem so tenuous. This facility, which I called 'feeling' acts much faster than reason and seems to process vast amounts of data in parallel rather than sequentially like logical thought. As such it is hard to put into words, the words chosen tend to be feeling words, and the process is more akin to Art than Science.

The distinction between this process and what I call 'thinking', 'reason' or 'logic' is very close to the distinction that is sometimes made between 'right brain' and 'left brain' processes. So we could define the distinction between Magic and Science as follows: "both Science and Magic seek to explore and operate upon the observed universe, but Magic gives final authority to right brain processing, while Science gives final authority to left brain processing".

Returning to the book's main argument, I suggest that the proper study of Magic could help us to understand and use these primitive survival skills to better advantage. In our civilised world we have demoted half our data processing abilities because their main value seems to be to cope with just the sort of sudden, unpredictable situations which we try to eliminate from our civilised world. Science is the process by which we try to eliminate the unpredictable. Magic is the process by which we could try to woo the unpredictable, and it is a great way to restore value to these lost processing skills.

The practice and study of Magic can make us a lot less silly about feelings and hunches.

9

CHAPTER TWO
Examples of different forms of Magic

At this point, it becomes necessary to describe a selection of techniques which would lie in the 'Magic' direction of the diagram and which are recognised and practiced at the present time. This is necessary in order to make it clear that Magic as here defined does in fact accord with the activities popularly associated with that word. On the other hand, there is a danger in picking a few topics from the vast range of Magical practices and attempting to outline them in a few words: it is the danger of fragmenting the subject once again.

This fragmentation goes against the spirit of Magic, for one of the qualities which distinguishes feeling from logic is the former's ability to process simultaneously a wide range of observations. In studying the following examples in greater depth, you will notice a tendency for Magic to take a broader and more inclusive view than the concentrated view of Science.

In this sense, we find a very interesting analogy of Magical thought in the cinema. Imagine the closing scenes of a tragic film the scenes of strife and struggle rushing to a closeup climax of agony-filled faces, then with a sweep of finale music and the camera slowly receding from the scene, a wider and further view fills the screen and the hero is now just a diminishing figure in a larger pattern of sunset scenery. The cinema's magic evokes a surge of emotion in its audience, be it sympathy or nausea.

Here Art and Magic are in accord while Science and Religion are still quibbling over the detailed rights and wrongs of the earlier action. In fact the first symptoms of Magic noticed in any system are often that it views a pattern too wide to be admitted by Science.

A curious note to the above illustration: a very academic rationalist took exception to it when shown the first edition of this book. He claimed that the example was dishonest because it played on different meanings of the word 'magic'. He had failed to notice the reversion to the lower case 'm' to distinguish other magics from the word as defined in this book. It is hard to be totally consistent without the assistance of a professional proof reader, but this text does aim to drop the upper case initials when a more accepted usage is implied.

We will start with a system closer to the Sciences. Astrology is largely founded on observation: feeling, though indispensable in interpretation, comes second. Astrology views events on earth in the larger pattern of the movements of the heavenly bodies. It asserts that, on the birth of any project, it would be as unrealistic to ignore the positions of the planets as it would be to ignore the immediate environment. In particular, we have Natal Astrology where the project in question is the first moment of separate existence of a human being, that is its 'first breath'. The pattern, or 'horoscope', of that moment is studied in the light of past experience, and it is used as a plan of the individual's being, and of its future development.

In scoffing at systems of Magic, it is common practice to overlook the importance of observation to them. In the case of astrology, the 'light of past experience' does not mean 'dead traditions'. In any group of astrologers, you will hear lively discussion of personal observations as to what characteristics 'go with' certain planetary positions. Indeed this answers the question "what do the astrologers do when a new planet is discovered?" They look out for consistent events when the planet is in key positions, and they look back at old horoscopes to see if the new planet adds any meaning to the old pattern.

Another problem which worries those who are ignorant of astrological technique is that of the relationships between the astrological signs — Aries, Taurus etc — and the precession of the equinox. The label 'Aries' still covers the first twelfth part of the zodiac even though it no longer coincides completely with the pattern of fixed stars also bearing that label, This is especially disconcerting for those who assume a causal theory of radiating influence from the stars; what they overlook is the corresponding evolution over the centuries of the interpretation of the astrological signs. Although this evolution is of about the correct speed to match the progression of the equinoxes, it should not be assumed that it merely amounts to a rotation so that the present day interpretation of Aries is now equal to the old interpretation of Taurus. We do not find that Spring is occurring earlier in the year as the equinoxes progress, so accordingly the interpretation of Aries is still largely based on the idea of initiative or first growth; and so on with the other signs in their cyclical relationship to Aries.

Some astrologers like to see themselves as Scientists, and quote the increasing importance of statistical analysis to their system. To some astrologers, statistics is as important as it is to some economists — so why not admit astrology to be a Science? Because astrology does not depend upon a causal link between the planets and the earth, the lack of a causal link is a break in the chain of logic — ie it is not logic. Feeling does not need that causal link. As a Scientist, the economist should use statistics to indicate correlations which can then be explored for causal links before proceeding further. If he omits that stage and relies on statistical correlation alone, he is slipping into Magic. Myself, I would be happier to admit sociology and psychology to the Magic sector than to place astrology in the Science sector.

Tarot divination is a system where feeling plays a much larger part relative to observation. Whereas the astrologer looks at his client's life as the smaller event in the larger context of cosmic patterns, the tarot reader studies a smaller event (ie the resultant order of a pack of shuffled tarot cards) in the larger context of his client's life.

The cards bear complicated pictorial symbols. Although the final spread is simpler than a horoscope — that is to say, there are fewer possibilities for interaction — the original symbols are far more complicated than the astrological ones. Thus the statistical method of almost pure observation does not lend itself to the learning of the tarot pack. Instead, it is necessary to feel your way around the symbols by meditation, and to supplement that meditation by observation of analogies in everyday life. Thus you learn what cards 'go with' what characteristic patterns in life.

I myself had difficulty interpreting tarot spreads at first. It was only after I had used them as prompts for telling bed-time stories to my baby that I formed a working relationship with the symbols. I used to lay four cards face down and turn them over one by one, making up a story as I did so. It was easy because it felt like 'play'. In this way I stopped 'trying to see meaning' but simply allowed the pictures to stimulate my imagination — and that way I learnt to interpret divinatory spreads.

In Ritual Magic, we learn to form attributions both by meditating and observing, but instead of passively studying the state of affairs in order to prophesy — as does the diviner — we deliberately set up an unnatural concentration of appropriate factors in order to precipitate a desired event — a parallel with a laboratory experiment.

In theory, any symbol system could be chosen. In practice, it is more likely to be based on the Cabala than pure astrology, but I will invent an astrological example as it is more likely to refer to symbols known to some degree by the reader.

Let us say that 'worldly success' is desired. What epitomises worldly success in the horoscope? Perhaps Sun in Leo on the mid-heaven with good aspects especially from Jupiter and Venus? Perhaps therefore we will have Jupiter and Venus in their own signs, ie Sagittarius and Libra respectively? There are many other things to look for — support from the Moon, ie the public, and from Saturn for a firm foundation — but I will oversimplify for the sake of clarity.

Ideally you wait for a time when every planet is perfectly placed; practically this is impossible, so you have to compromise. Let us imagine that Sun, Venus and Jupiter are well placed as above, but that Mercury is badly placed in Pisces and receives a bad aspect from Neptune but a good one from Mars in Capricorn, and that Saturn is terribly placed and has no redeeming good aspects at all.

If nothing can be done about Saturn's bad influence, it had better be cut out. (I admit that 'influence' is not the ideal word — there is no assumption of a causal influence here. The 'bad influence' is a bad influence on the pattern — just as a heavy moustache might be a bad influence upon the composition of the Mona Lisa. So read this passage as one might read an art criticism.) Thus the temple furnishings should omit the use of black or Saturnine colours, and the rite should include actions and phrases to banish Saturn's influence from the place of working. In later life, this might correspond to a need to leave old people, traditions and delays out of your plans for success.

The bad influence of Mercury and Neptune all indicate a danger from treachery, so do we banish these two as well? Here is a decision: the more we banish, the less of the whole picture is left to support us. Better therefore to try to deflect their influence via Mars' good aspect.

Mars in Capricorn is a severe position — in later life, it might corre-spond to the deflection of trickery by taking a hard, even cruel line. So where the furnishings reflect Mercury, by tradition for example in the magician's sandals and the words spoken, we will try to align them with the helpful Martian element. For example, to protect the feet (Pisces) from. treachery (Mercury) while dancing the ritual, we will make sure the sandals are securely fastened with iron (Mars) buckles.

As can be imagined from these examples, the possible precautions are endless. But what do they add up to? The Magician now has a time and a place which is perfectly attuned to arouse in his own thinking the full spirit of worldly success with the result that he will achieve during his ritual the feeling of complete worldly success.

In this sense, he has basically done no more than the host who plans a party: a place and time are chosen, and the place is decorated so as to play up its amusing and party-like aspects, and to cover up the grimmer aspects by tidying them away. Thus the good party spirit is invoked to the gathering. But that is not the end of it, for the party will provide happy memories and will lead to new friendships and further invitations. Nowadays there is also the 'magical' possibility of capturing the spirit of the event in some photographs, or a tape recording. If this is done, the host will be able to revive the occasion for years ahead, bringing out the photos to show to friends and once more they are all laughing.

The Ritual Magician too likes to capture his spirit in a talisman. His system predates photography or the tape recorder; he will prepare an 'amulet' as carefully as he decorated his room. Perhaps the amulet will take the form of a disc of gold (Sun) supported in a ring of tin (Jupiter) and on a copper (Venus) chain. On it will be inscribed symbols — the horoscope of the moment, for example — which completely summarise his ritual. After the ceremony, this talisman will be carefully stored away to be produced and used only when the spirit of worldly success is most needed. Like the perfect host, he knows the talisman or photos would lose their effect if just left around the place for twenty-four hours every day.

Nowhere is the interplay between observation and feeling more vividly seen than in the study of alchemy. Alchemy is the method by which substances are brought to perfection, or at least a 'higher' state by first breaking them down to their simplest parts and then rebuilding them. The process of brainwashing and re-indoctrination is an example of this method — but alchemy is more popularly associated either with the conversion of base metals into gold, or else with the spiritual perfecting of the individual himself.

The alchemist studies natural processes minutely and describes them in greater detail than the Scientist. If the putrefaction of some mixture becomes so objectionable that it depresses the alchemist, he will note that fact in his alchemical diary, whereas the Scientist would omit his own subjective depression as being irrelevant. As a result, the alchemist learns more about himself as he studies nature, and conversely more about nature as he studies himself. He will note that a grain or seed cannot realise itself, ie grow into a plant, in the dry state; it must be buried and soaked until it 'rots'. Similarly, a brew does not turn straight from barley into beer without passing through the decomposing effect of fermentation. On the other hand, he will note how unqualified success renders people inflexible: the times of genuine development tend to follow the times of failure, of decomposition and of rebuilding. These separate observations will come together in the alchemist's mind and he will deduce practical modes of action in his own life.

Here we are approaching what might be called the 'purer' or more abstract forms of Magic. There are occultists who refrain from the paraphernalia and deliberate strivings of Ritual Magic and yet who bring about desired events by a careful manipulation of subtle principles which are deduced from feeling their way around observed facts. For example, they might note the same moment of time described above for Ritual Magic and use it to precipitate success, not by a dramatic ritual but by the rather more mundane arrangement of circumstances for that day — so that all possible other interpretations of those astrological aspects are rendered unlikely, and that the success of a particular project is the only remaining channel for the fulfillment of those aspects.

The Magic of Austin Spare is the example of such a 'pure' system. He admits the subjectivity of our beliefs and desires, then extends this subjectivity by indicating the extent to which even our surroundings

and circumstances can be seen as a projection of forgotten or unconscious beliefs and desires. So to admit and neutralise those beliefs
which limit us is to alter one's circumstances for the better.
Alternatively, if we can replace the destroyed belief with a new one
suitable for a desired state (eg replace an unconscious belief that 'I was
just born unlucky' by one that 'I am bound to make it someday') and
we can succeed in moving that belief away from the ineffective
conscious state and down into the effective unconscious state, then
we can alter our circumstances. Here we are close to the alchemical
idea of first reducing to simplicity before rebuilding. Spare's system is
strongly akin to the principles of much New Age teaching, but the
practice looks very different.

The handful of examples that have been given must not be seen as a
survey of Magic, nor as a full explanation of what each example is
about. Its purpose is, on the one hand, to provide illustrations of how
diverse in outcome the combinations of observation and feeling can
be, for the sake of those who have no knowledge of Magic; and on
the other hand, to show that the original definition is found to cover
the whole range of Magical method, for the sake of those who already
have some knowledge of Magic and might therefore not be happy
with that definition.

*Magic processes data in parallel (ie as 'sympa-
thies') where Science would process data in
sequence (ie as 'causes').*
*Thus sympathetic Magic is the core of all Magic.
To invoke a god or spirit you bring together
qualities, objects and actions sympathetic to that
spirit. To precipitate an event you bring together
gods and spirits sympathetic to that event.*

CHAPTER 2A
Further examples

Around the time this book was first published the seeds were being sown of a new Magical current which became known as chaos magic. In fact this book had an important influence upon that current because it presented a comparatively clear and undogmatic overview of basic Magical principles, and that is very much what chaos magic is all about.

It should be growing clear by now that dogmatism has absolutely no place in Magic, whereas in Religion (and in Science as will be explained in Cap 3A) it has such a key role that it needs to be very carefully monitored. Simply because dogmatism has no place in Magic, it is traditionally welcomed in as guest of honour.

So a typical introduction to astrology might well begin with the dogmatic statement "We are, every one of us, under the influence of the stars..." even though a majority of astrologers think in terms of synchronicity or cycles rather than influences, and those who do work with an influence model are far more likely to use planetary than stellar influences.

Another Magical book might begin with a statement such as "Beyond the realm of the senses there exist dark forces which govern this world, mighty powers mastered by a priestly caste before the Fall using secret knowledge which has since been available to a select few who hold the keys to the most secret inner temples of the adepti..." Terrific stuff, and damn good Magic for those lucky enough to be able to swallow all that. Unfortunately for Magic, however, our Scientific education has somewhat constricted the throat against such stuff. Science values truth as highly as the finest wine — to be sipped not gulped — while Magic is more inclined to knock truth back with gusto and then concentrate on sipping at whatever experience then results.

Chaos magic allows for such modern sensibilities by putting the dogma through a blender. A typical eight word blender is "Let us adopt a belief system in which..." and then follows the above crap about dark forces. The word "paradigm" makes a useful blender for over-Scientific sensibilities. What the chaos magician is putting into practice is Austin Spare's principle of acting "as if". As will be explained in my example in Chapter 3A, the correct approach to a Magical theory or model is not to seek to disprove it as one would with a Scientific theory, but to see if you can convince yourself that it is true by acting as if it was true. If this results in the theory 'working', then you rejoice in it as a practical tool. What you do not do is assume therefore that it must be 'true' in any significant sense. It is actually better Magic to keep the discovery to oneself than to evangelise or announce it publicly as if it was a Religious or Scientific truth.

By spelling out so clearly the "as if" process, and wrapping it in semi-Scientific terms such as 'belief systems' or 'paradigms of choice', chaos magic provides almost bomb-proof defence against the sort of delusions which used to befall inexperienced dabblers in Magic. Chaos magic is, in effect, the safest Magical system there is. Paradoxically, however, it has gained a red hot reputation for being the most dangerous, sinister and crazed form of Magical madness extant. How can this be?

I believe this is a simple matter of human psychology. What happens when you force motorcyclists to wear helmets and protective clothing? The answer is that they go faster. And when cars are provided with seat belts, crumple zones, better tyres and air bags — people drive even faster still. It is precisely the bomb-proof intellectual basis of chaos magic which makes it so secure and which therefore tempts its practitioners to rush in where angels fear to tread — invoking every weird and awesome entity in the pantheon and inventing even weirder ones to feed the need for speed!

To pursue chaos magic is to ride the comet's tail — and it is great fun. Having such a shameless, wicked reputation is even greater fun.

The remarks on tarot divination can, of course, be generalised to embrace the runes, geomancy symbols, tea-leaves or any other divinatory system.

Reduced to essence it is this: we seek an answer to a question and we believe that there is a greater intelligence which knows the answer better than us (and we may choose to believe that the intelligence lies within us or without). In theory we could simply sit and meditate and hope to speak directly to that intelligence. In fact the signals are very weak, so weak that we choose to amplify them by superimposing random noise in the form of shuffled cards, yarrow stalks or the swirlings of tea leaves — examples which seem to deliver about the right level of noise to resonate with psychic data. Scientists deny the value of this amplification technique even though they find it practiced in nature, where random noise is used to resonate with weak signals and make them easier to detect.

The purest form of divination, in this sense, is that practiced by Chaos magicians when they use a tv screen as a 'crystal ball'. The tv is switched to an un-tuned channel to deliver a screenfull of random video noise, and the Magician gazes at this screen until the mind begins to discern images in the chaos.

Feng Shui is another example I will add to the list as it has become more popular in the West in recent years. The very essence of Feng Shui, as I see it, is to ask 'does this location feel right and, if not, what adjustments can we make to improve the feeling', coupled with a presumption that getting this right feeling in the environment will go with corresponding greater success or harmony in life and business. As such, Feng Shui is very much a Magical process.

In practice, however, Feng Shui became highly systematised with rules and correspondences. The traditional Feng Shui compass looks like a precision Scientific instrument until you analyse the way it is used. Superficially, then, Feng Shui might appear almost Scientific to the lay person. How can this happen?

I believe it is a manifestation of a cultural evolution which is described in Chapter 3A. Times change and different ways of thinking come and go. When Religion is dominant, it tends to overlay Magical practice and you get all the prayers, psalms and conjurations of the traditional grimoires. When rationalism takes over there is an urge to systematise and try to 'pin down' this feeling of 'what goes with what', and we inherit the highly complex tables of cabalistic correspondence, and the rules of Feng Shui.

This is another example to illustrate that the four ways of thinking described in this book are four directions, and not tidy categories. Much of what I call "Magic" presents itself as pseudo-science or pseudo-religion because those are the forms in which it was accepted in the past. But if you strip away appearances and techniques and look at the basic thinking behind them, you recognise them as Magic in my terms.

From Feng Shui we come to another phenomenon which has emerged since, and partly because of, the first edition of this book. The 'New Age' is a subject of such breadth that it is not so much a branch of Magic as a a parallel to it. On the one hand it might seem to be just another word for Magic, on the other hand it can appear as a rival system of thought quite opposed in spirit. For this reason I am leaving the discussion of the New Age to Appendix B.

CHAPTER THREE
How Magic diverges from Science

So far, Magic has been described without reference to 'supernatural forces', 'higher worlds' or 'powers of darkness'. The danger in omitting such references is the danger of presenting Magic to look too much like 'common sense'.

It is not that there is not a very large element of 'common sense' in Magic, it is rather the way in which we tackle naked common sense that makes it desirable to cloak it in mystique.

Until one is practiced in self observation, it is easy to forget the extent to which Scientific thought dominates present day thinking, and thus often manages to rule it. A very natural twentieth century reaction to a meeting with common sense is "can't we tackle this more scientifically?" The result is a proliferation of ludicrous or ineffectual '-ologies', '-onics' and '-etics'. Therefore it is necessary to explain in some detail how Magic diverges from other systems — in particular from Science as the most familiar to us — in order to explain the futility of attempting to 'approach Magic scientifically'.

The first difference to note between Magic and Science stems from the subjectivity of feeling when compared with logic. This is not to say that feeling is utterly independent of objective influence: the wine you sample at the wine merchant is liable to taste better for the knowledge that it is the most expensive wine on their list. Science recognises an objective body of truth, or at least accepted dogma, and not even the most consistent work will be admitted by Scientists unless it has links with this accepted truth. This is another reason why astrology cannot be called a Science.

You do not find a Scientist gazing in scornful disbelief at a heap of snow white sodium chloride crystals saying "no-one can kid me there's chlorine in that stuff." Chemical theory says there is chlorine, and that is that. It is a common mistake to approach Magic in the same gullible spirit. It is easy to read in a Magical text that sandalwood is a correct perfume for invocations of Venus, and to assume therefore that sandalwood somehow 'contains' Venus in the way that sodium chloride contains chlorine. With this sort of belief, the dabbler will mechanically re-enact an empty ritual.

He may have some success. Although the attribution of Venus to sandalwood is not as rigid as the chemist's dogma, it does have the power of the wine merchant's quiet reference to the price of the wine you are raising to your lips. So it is possible for the link between Venus and sandalwood to be formed in your mind simply through an awe of your sources of reference. However a more correct approach would be to use the reference as a guide and to supplement the very necessary awe with personal experiment and a refining of the attribution with such subjective observations as "Yuck: the combination of sandalwood and sweaty armpits really turns me off."

More commonly we see such errors when people approach astrology in insufficient depth. It is easy to conclude that "Venus equals my love life" and to make a lot of erroneous predictions on that idea. In fact the astrological significance of Venus relates also to art, social pleasures, women, possessions and many other subjects. Conversely, you will find essential facets of love life referred to other planets, eg passion to Mars, moods to the Moon. So the correct approach to this extraordinary hotch-potch of attributions is not the dogmatic 'Venus equals love life', but rather a gradual accumulation of experience and reflection until the diverse elements begin to fit together, to 'feel right'. Only when that stage is reached is prediction worth attempting, and it is done by recognising the wide range of possible interpretations of any one aspect, and allowing the multitude of other factors to play upon that range until a most likely outcome is indicated.

A less direct manifestation of this error is seen in the mistaken belief (prevalent among journalists) that a collection of stories of inexplicable events amounts to a 'case for Magic', or conversely that stories of unsuccessful laboratory tests on psychic phenomena amount to a 'case against Magic'. Such stories can only sway the belief of those who are in a particular state of half-way doubt. The test of a Magical theory is not whether it fits a hotch-potch of 'objective facts' thrown at you from hostile sources, but whether it fits your own experience.

So in place of the 'accepted body of Scientific truth', Magic's truth is ultimately subjective, even though members of any one Magical school may share many elements of that truth. In view of this fact, it seems paradoxical that the subjective Magical truths should be much less time-dependent than the objective Scientific truths: the early twentieth century Magicians who tended to talk in terms of 'etheric vibrations' and the 'fourth dimension' were still happy to use Renaissance, mediaeval or even classical textbooks, whereas Scientists' textbooks are liable to be obsolete within a decade.

It is tempting to note the obsolesence of Scientific theory as reason not to 'believe in' Science — "if every past Scientific theory has now been proved false in some degree, then we can deduce an extreme likelihood that today's Scientific theories must also be false." The problem with that argument is that it requires acceptance of the latest theories in order to prove that previous theories were false, and so to deduce that the latest theories should not have been accepted. Instead I simply use the word 'progressive' to distinguish Scientific theories from Magical ones — see Chapter Seven.

The second important difference between Magical and Scientific thought lies in the attitude to causality. A primitive Magician of the kind imagined in earlier examples might well be baffled as to how the pedestrian processes of logic could ever come to be applied usefully to operations upon the real world. If he pursued his inquiries, he would perhaps conclude that the Scientific mind had solved the problem by a process of 'projection'. It was projecting the logical links of its thought processes onto the physical world and thus observing a series of links, ie 'causes', in that world. A more sophisticated Magical explanation would refer to the congruence of Microcosm and Macrocosm, ie 'inner' and 'outer' worlds, and conclude that: a) because it is possible for our minds to reach conclusions by a series of logical linked steps, b) therefore it is natural to assume that a similar principle or 'causality' can operate in the physical world.

In this century we are heavily steeped in Scientific thought. Even though this does not mean we are all good Scientists, it certainly does mean that we find it hard to understand how other ways of thought could operate. This is particularly true when we approach a Magician and find that he has no interest in causality. A practicing Magician has no interest in the philosophical problems which torment the Scientist who asks "Are you sure it was your Magic that cured her?

How do you know it was not just coincidence?" Such speculation is irrelevant to the Magician. He did the spell, she was cured. If it was a coincidence, it doesn't matter just so long as he can bring about such coincidences.

In fact such perfect Magical thought is rare; in the present age, the Magicians are inclined to limit themselves to some degree under the influence of the idea of causality. As is usually the case, their results are in accord with the limitations of their thinking. In past ages, Religious thought dominated with its emphasis on morality, and accounts survive of miracles which defy causality but bow to morality — gold coins, for example, which materialise from thin air but do their owner no good unless spent upon charity. Nowadays the Magician will find morality becoming less of a limitation, but he is unlikely to find that his spells will defy causality — eg instead of materialising gold coins, he might have 'luck' on a state lottery.

Instead of defying causality, modern Magic tends to stretch it slowly, within the operator's subjectively conceived world. A typical example of this is seen in the different attitudes that are held towards divination as a student Magician progresses. The first theory adopted is usually some form of direct causality; a belief that there might be rays from the planets which affect us, or that the impressive symbols of the tarot pack so mesmerise us that we will tend to make the predictions come true by our own belief in them. Such a theory is the natural choice of an inexperienced modern, but it tends to come unstuck as practical experience is gained — by this I mean working experience, not just a trek round the different consultant astrologers. The results and the methods used both diverge from that basic theory.

A typical 'second generation' Magical theory of divination is that the unconscious part of the brain is vastly greater than the conscious part, and therefore has terrific potential for computation. Thus, if a problem of the future is presented in appropriate symbolic terms, the most likely outcome can be computed by the unconscious. So the necessary symbols for divination should be those sufficiently vague or inflexible for the unconscious to be able to project its conclusions into them — to be read by the groping consciousness. But again working experience will tend to erode such a theory, not by actively defying it, but rather by slowly stretching the apparent powers of the unconscious until they pass the bounds of our belief; that is, they present us with an unconscious more powerful than can be tolerated, by our other beliefs about the structure of the brain. After that, the next generation of theory is of an acausal connective principle, eg synchronicity.

The main lesson from this for the progressive Magician is that Magic, like Science, is reluctant to shatter our basic beliefs. Therefore, it is desirable to choose the most flexible possible beliefs for our working, because such beliefs allow more room for things to happen.

Because we are so steeped in the idea of causality, it is correct that I should approach the Magical position from a starting point of causality, even though it is ultimately irrelevant. So in answer to the question "what does the Magician have in place of an idea of causality?", I will answer that the Magician does not deny a connection between events, but rather assumes that every event is connected to every other. This assumption makes the search for a chain of causes ridiculous: the links are too numerous and complex for analysis.

Of course, this assumption is ultimately true even in Scientific theory: a flea jumping in the most distant galaxy exerts a possible gravitational effect on this world which could be expressed mathematically even though it is too small ever to be measured. However, reason plus observation cannot as a team handle more than a small finite number of factors.

As an illustration of this, it is often instructive to consider how a Scientist analyses a successful Magical operation. Let us say a Magician who wished for worldly success went to some trouble to obtain gold and other equipment and performed the ritual outlined previously, and that he achieved a remarkable up-turn in his fortunes soon after. The Scientist, if he accepts the bare facts, is likely to argue on lines such as the following. Either it is pure 'coincidence' or else:

Scientist: "Well presumably you were held back by some sort of inferiority complex, which was eased by your belief that you now had Magic power on your side."

Magician: "But why would my ritual have such a quick effect on the complex, where psychiatrists had failed?"

Scientist: "I suppose it was because it forced you to get off your backside and actually do something symbolic about your condition. Under the psychiatrist you were a passive patient."

Magician: "And how could the mere easing of a complex cause me to have become so successful?"

Scientist: "Because you then went about your work in a positive way, and did it better."

Magician: "But my boss promoted me within the same week, before my better work had time to become apparent."

Scientist: "Well I suppose it's possible that your more confident bearing subtly attracted his attention."

Magician: "But why would my promotion have been pushed forward by seniors who had never even met me?"

Scientist: "It does happen you know that a successful person gains a sort of momentum. The good impression you've made on your boss, and others, is subtly reflected in their descriptions or memoranda about you. When asked to list candidates, your name comes first to his mind, and therefore is remembered by others; and so on, once the ball is rolling."

Of course this Scientist is rapidly ceasing to talk like a Scientist — Magic has that effect on rationalists! But this process of trying to approach a feeling-judgement by a series of small causal links can be quite a useful exercise for a Magician, and also a possible approach to the understanding and trust of feeling.

In view of this example, you might think that a Scientist could easily come to terms with Magic by using such an approach. But this is far from the case, for if we invert the example with respect to time and present a Magician who is *planning* a Magical operation and *advocating* it by the same listing of the possible causal benefits, then we find that as the suggested causal links grow more and more tenuous there will come a point where the Scientist thinks that the planned operation is ridiculously optimistic.

If we accept that everything is linked with everything else, then between any two events which 'feel' associated, there will be an infinite series of possible causal links which can be discovered in this way. As each link becomes more and more tenuous, we could symbolise those links by a series of numbers 1/2, 1/4, 1/8, 1/16 etc. Now this series 1/2 + 1/4 + 1/8 +... if added indefinitely tends to the limit total of 1. This fact is what is perceived by the feeling of the Magician whereas the Scientist is analogous to the person who stops at, say, 1/512 because it is "surely too small to make any difference."

The method of Science demands that we stop after a finite number of factors have been considered in relation to a problem, and ignore for the time being all further factors, But in Magic, the end point is sensed and 'achieved' through a seemingly irrelevant ritual.

Of course, this example is poor because the actual series 1/2 + 1/4 + 1/8 + . . . is a series of like terms — real numbers — and so could be handled by the Scientist using the mathematical methods for convergent series. But in real life, the series are of unlike terms, eg personal psychological effects, resultant effects on associates, resultant sociological effects, economic effects, etc.

The distaste that a Scientist has for Magical method also arises at a deeper level than that of a mere rejection of insufficient causal links: it arises on account of the previously mentioned dichotomy between the Scientist's objective world and the subjective Magical one. I was once told that the basic objection which the Inquisition had to Galileo's theories was not, as is popularly supposed, because he claimed that the earth went round the sun, but rather because he insisted that this was an absolute and objective fact which really happened 'out there'. In other words, he was granting to a piece of knowledge the absoluteness which was considered only proper for a God. This absolute belief appears to be basic to Scientific thinkers and makes it very hard for twentieth century man to accept the more convenient and adaptable beliefs of Magicians.

Let us say that a Magician has invoked Venus in a ritual to secure the love of a chosen girl, and that he has been stupid enough to let a Scientist know of his action. As would be expected, the Scientist would want to know how a planet could affect the love of a girl, and an argument would begin on the lines described above: the Scientist admitting that the ritual might boost the Magician's confidence and make him more attractive, but not admitting much more.

But if the argument is pursued, it will be found that the two thinkers are not in fact arguing about the same Venus, even though they can both point to the same heavenly body as they use the word. To the Scientist, Venus is an objective reality, a vast mass of mineral like our Earth though millions of miles distant. Although he will admit that we do not yet know everything about Venus, he does believe that it is a real and absolute object, and that all knowledge is out there in physical form waiting to be discovered. Therefore he is irritated to hear the Magician's apparently woolly associations of Venus with women, love, copper, green and other irrelevant human-centric qualities. To the Scientist, these attributions are a relic of a time when uneasy ignorance was disguised behind imagination.

To the Magician, this is all absurdly, though disarmingly, idealis-tic. The Scientist sees the universe as an absolute and real world of Truth, partly discovered and largely still to be discovered, and he crit-icises the Magician's view of the world as being a subjective version of the true world which has been distorted by the Magician's own imagination and gullibility. To the Magician, this Scientist's opinion is indistinguishable from that of those Religious minds who declare the world we live in to be only an evil illusion hiding the real world beyond.

Although the Scientist is so sure of the reality of that lump of matter in space, he is never likely to know it through his own direct experience: instead he accepts the word of authorities whom he considers to be reliable. To the Magician, this is all very idealistic but much less trustworthy than those attributions of Venus which have been previously discovered, implanted or encouraged in his own mind. Instead of quoting distant authorities, he is describing what he knows well through experiments in the 'laboratory' of his own mind. As said before: it is wrong to think that the Magician blindly accepts the attributions he reads in old textbooks; unless such attributions are accepted and 'charged' by the Magician, they are liable to be useless. Although you may hear of dabblers who get results through the mechanical performance of an old ritual, such workings do no more deserve the title of Magic than does an inadvertently ignited stick of dynamite deserve to be described as a 'Scientific Investigation of Detonation'.

Let us conveniently accept the Scientist's assertion that all thought processes are chemical and electrical reactions within the brain. In that case, even the Scientist's concept of Venus is only to be experienced in the form of such reactions. The Magician's self-esteem, his charm, his confidence — or whatever more subtle characteristics are needed to attract the desired girl — are also part of the same complex electro-chemical structure, as is the experience of the very girl desired. Is it really to be believed that all the separate electrical and chemical impulses are contained within the same small lump of matter and yet in no way interact with one another? What is so strange, therefore, in stirring up one complex of associations, ie Venus, in order to influence another, ie the girl as experienced?

There are many people whom I would describe as Scientific thinkers but who would themselves scoff at any such label, merely wishing to be described as 'down to earth'. Such people would ask: why go to all that trouble to attract that girl by working on complicated symbols? Wouldn't it be simpler just to work on the girl herself?

If it was simpler to work on the girl herself, then the Magician should have chosen to do so, for in Magic less so than in Science there is no virtue in doing this in a roundabout way simply in order to experiment. But the questioner shows a typically Scientific fallacy when he assumes it would be simple to work on the girl herself. The Magician is in fact being much more realistic when he admits that even the simplest girl is vastly more complex than any symbol system he can devise. Even though to the Scientist the ramifications of the Magician's Venus symbolism may seem desperately more involved than his basic idea of 'the girl', in fact the purpose of such Magical systems as astrology and the cabala is to provide the necessary language in order to simplify the confusion of symbols.

The Scientific method is hopelessly out of depth in the real life business of seduction. The fact that Scientists ever succeed at it can only be proof that the heat of emotion is sufficient to banish the Scientific Spirit, and to allow the unconscious Magical abilities to take over.

The 'down to earth' man would argue that both Scientific thought and Magical ritual were irrelevant to seduction all they could ever, do is to give the man confidence so that 'It' could work unhindered. The Magician would gladly agree, insisting only that 'It' was Magic.

So we see again how the Magician thinks in the Microcosm and the Scientist in the Macrocosm, and we see the danger of interpreting the terms Microcosm and Macrocosm too unsubtly as the 'inner world' and the 'outer world '. It is wrong to think that Magic somehow ignores the physical world — it merely views it in a different manner and one which will be expanded in a later chapter. This difference of viewpoint is not easily understood by the Scientist, and its manifestation continually surprises.

For example, we are so used to thinking of the universe as a vast unexplored mass of facts, and of Scientific discovery as the harvesting process which goes out and collects these facts to feed our expanding growing knowledge, that the Magical view of this same process seems absurd. The Magical view is that the whole universe is already explored — by the imagination. Everything that is necessary, and more, is already known. To the Magician, Science or any other system of practical discovery is not so much a harvest as a slaughter: once upon a time the Moon was the left eye of Horus, a wicked woman, green cheese, an inhabited world like ours, the abode of the dead . . . in fact an infinity of different things according to our psychic needs at the time. Science has cut down most of the possibilities leaving only those which start with the idea of a sterile lump of mineral. In my own view, it is still possible for the Moon to be a rich source of diamonds. In due course, Science is sure to kill that one too. In this manner, Science is not adding to our world as the Magician would see it; on the contrary, it is clearing it in order to make us feel more secure. So the irrational feeling which haunts some of us — the feeling that Science is shrinking the world and making it more boring and empty — is possibly a betrayal of a suppressed inclination towards the Magical way of thought.

As was earlier suggested, there is a large element of common sense in Magic, and at first glance its techniques might seem as though they could even be compatible with Scientific thought. In order to dispel that idea, the basic ways in which Magic and Science diverge have been illustrated at length.

Science, rather than Art or Religion, was chosen as a comparison. because we are all to some extent biased towards the Scientific manner of thought in this century, and so at least these illustrations are more likely to be understood from that angle. This same bias also means that we are more likely to attempt to fit Magic into the Scientific way of thought, because the latter is natural to us. It was therefore necessary to show the ultimate impossibility of such attempts. I am not moralising — there is nothing wrong in trying to be Scientific about Magic, in fact the attempt could teach the experimenter a lot about himself. But it would be a mistake for him to believe that he was doing Magic in the attempt, or learning anything positive about Magic.

The journalistic ideas of a 'war' between, say, Science and Religion or Magic and Science is rubbish in these terms. Science, Art, Religion and Magic can happily co-exist without impinging upon each other. Like Earth, Air, Fire and Water — or better still North, South, East and West — you can combine or confuse them as much as you like, but it will always be possible to separate out these vectors once more, untouched by each other's proximity.

CHAPTER 3A
Cycles of thought

In the last chapter, and again in later chapters, several key distinctions are drawn between Science and Magic. In Scientific terms these could define a relationship between the two, summarised as a table of distinctions along these lines —

FACTOR	SCIENCE	MAGIC
Aim	Truth	Wholeness
Objectivity	Yes	No
Causality	Yes	No
Belief	Conditional	Unconditional
Truth	Absolute	Relative

— and so on.

Relationship by distinction is a particularly Scientific notion of relationship. As Magical thinking relies more on spacial, pattern recognition abilities, it is more inclined to ask where Magic 'stands relative to' Science. This is a different approach to relationship. Although this version of relationship may be too woolly for strict Scientific analysis, many Scientists would still choose to answer the question, and they would often do so by saying that Magic was 'a primitive forerunner of Science'.

This was certainly what I was encouraged to believe in my childhood in the 1950s: that Magic was originally a prehistoric, uneducated attempt to make sense of, or control, the environment. It was suggested that Magic then evolved in two different directions: towards the spiritual discipline of Religion and to the technological discipline of Science. This belief meant that any resurgence of interest in Magic could be seen as dangerous or at least threatening — because it was evidence of regression towards our less civilised past.

This view of Magic seems to be making a comeback. In early 1997 Richard Dawkins gave a lecture on BBC TV in which he expressed misgivings about public irrationalism. He drew attention to programmes like *The X*

Files and the way that the media seemed to be encouraging unscientific thinking rather than working actively to guide public debate along more rational lines. In the same week the BBC radio programme *The Moral Maze* picked up his theme. It was clear that the panel did not approve of what was happening. They too seemed perplexed that today's society, with its education and ready accessibility of Scientific ideas and methods, should be so susceptible to such unscientific 'delusions'.

When I heard Dawkins addressing the popularity of New Age ideas at the Cheltenham Literary Festival, what struck me was the strength of his feelings on the subject. There seemed to be something stronger than reason driving his distaste for the rise of New Age pseudo science. I concluded that, in the terms of my recent volume of essays — *What I Did In My Holidays* — Dawkins had evoked a demon. Like myself, he is a champion of the notion that ideas can replicate and evolve within the ecology of human culture in a manner akin to the Darwinian model. The demon he had evoked was the apparent fear that New Age ideas might now be proving fitter to survive than his own ideas. Having demoted 'goodness' or 'godliness' and replaced it with 'fitness' as the key determinant, he has to face the possibility that Science's 'Truth' might not be enough to save it from extinction. He can thus appear as a tribal shaman dancing a devil dance to protect his mind-children from a stronger foe.

But even without accepting Dawkins' and my beliefs about the evolution of ideas, some people still seem disturbed that a rational culture could return to Magical modes of thinking. As the original edition of this book pointed out in the early 1970s, however, this is not only ok, it is perfectly normal. Magic does not precede Science — it generally follows after it.

I first became aware of this in my own life, having evolved from pre-teen piety, through teenage skepticism to an interest in the occult at university. Far from experiencing these occult studies as a degeneration of my Scientific education, a backwards slide into atavism, they seemed like an expansion of my mental horizons, as growth beyond the skeptical Scientism of my teens. Nor did it begin with a withering of skepticism; on the contrary, that skepticism increased to the point where it turned upon the principles of Science itself: I witnessed Science itself failing to meet the standards of proof that were demanded of parascience.

So was this progression from Science towards Magic simply my personal aberration? No, because I had witnessed a similar, slower change in society between the 1950s and 60s: a change from a culture that was excited by Science towards one that was more excited by Magic. Again, Magic following upon Science and not vice versa. Nor was the 1960s unique as a popular Magical revival: a similar thing happened at the end of the nineteenth century, and again it was a reaction following triumphant Victorian Scientific materialism.

These observations and reflections lead to my theory of cycles of thought which I expand in this chapter — rather than deferring it to Chapter Nine as in the original SSOTBME. I do this in order to introduce a fuller example of a Magical theory in preparation for Chapter Seven. So the following description must be followed as a Magical theory, and not as a Scientific one — which is to say the reader must focus on verification rather than falsification.

VERIFICATION NOT FALSIFICATION IN MAGICAL THEORY

What follows is an example of a Magical theory.

It begins with an observation of mine own inner state, and the recognition of a cyclical pattern of development. (The pattern is said to be 'recognised' rather than 'discovered', because the latter would imply the more Scientific notion that it 'really existed', whereas Magic is less bothered whether it is true or imposed as long as it can be experienced.) I then go on to recognise a similar cyclical pattern occurring at several levels in society.

Several benefits are gained from this exercise, including: a sense of power from understanding the chaos of history; a sense of superior perception over Richard Dawkins to balance the recognition that he is a more successful writer than myself; and finally the provision of material for this book. (Recognition of these benefits helps define this as a Magical as opposed to an Artistic process.)

The process of pattern recognition requires us to lay aside the critical analytical faculty, but it does not require us to reject it outright. Once a pattern has been recognised you can always choose to analyse it, but there is little point in looking so closely that you no longer see the pattern. That is why I ask the reader to focus now on verification, not falsification.

Let me expand this difference. The sword or dagger is a magical symbol of the logic of Science — it contrasts with the cup as a magical symbol of the feeling of Magic. The former is about banishment and falsification, the latter about acceptance and confirmation. So when, for example, I describe the late 60s as a time of 'Magical revival' after the materialism of the 50s, you should adjust your vision of the 60s until you find a sense in which it did indeed feel like a Magical revival. Do not look for counter-arguments. Ignore for the time being the equal truth that a whole wave of 60s consumer technology had arrived — transistor radios, colour tvs etc — new technology which lay way out of reach in the supposedly materialistic 50s. The point was that such technology was now taken for granted, it did not excite us as Magic began to. Look instead at the fashionable interests — record covers covered with exotic magical imagery which was a direct reference to the earlier magical revival at the beginning of the century.

Try to see the truth in what I am saying rather than to test it for falsifiability — that is the correct approach to a Magical theory. While Scientists compete to disprove or reject ideas, Magicians compete to accept them. This approach worries rationalists who fear that such a gullible attitude must lead down a slippery slope into delusion. The Magical method is to act 'as if' a theory is correct until it has done its job, and only then to replace it with another theory. A theory only fails if it cannot take hold in the mind and allow one to act 'as if'. As long as this approach is carried out properly — with a Magician's understanding that the theory is being accepted only because it is 'working', not because it is 'true' — then there is little danger of delusion.

Where there is danger, it stems from lack of Magical understanding. Our empirical Scientific education inclines us to believe that if a theory is working then it is more likely to be 'true' — and such belief can indeed be dangerous.

This is another reason why I consider it important to re-issue this book: the real danger lies not so much in Magic as in people's misunderstanding, misapplication and denial of it.

A PERSONAL CYCLE

The extent to which a new-born babe is a blank slate or not is open to debate, nevertheless it is clear that its mind has had little time to build up inner resources of memory and prejudice. Compared with an older child, therefore, the baby is very much an observer, rather than intuitive. And it processes its observations by feeling rather than logic ('big soft pink things are to be sucked').

So we begin our lives as 'Magical' thinkers. By early childhood we have built up an inner world of memories which begins to overwhelm observation and shift the emphasis toward intuition, but we still have not mastered real logic. So we evolve into 'Artistic' thinking: a golden age when we live out myths of fairies and dragons and can believe in them *when we want to*: The armchair *is* a space ship when we play with it.

Around the pre-teen age this growing intuitive sense has overwhelmed feeling and the reasoning power is now in the ascendent. Still living off our rich inner worlds, we begin to wonder why things are as they are. This rather serious-minded phase of 'Religious' thinking lasts until the teenage years when logic grows to dominate intuition, and a growing awareness of the outside world moves us into 'Scientific' skepticism: 'just give me one good *reason* why I can't stay out all night,' demands the teenager.

To a rationalist the above is just a rather quaintly worded model of the evolution of thought through various primitive stages towards 'adult, rational thinking'. But I argue that this cycle does not stop at adolescence. I recall how my own observation grew so strong that I began to notice the flaws in Scientific thought and the areas of life it could not explain away: so I inclined toward Magical thinking as a student, at the age when so many of us become interested in the occult. During the early 20s we once more act out myths — the Young Man with Sports Car, the Newlyweds, etc. — until the 'saturn return' and the approaching age of 30 makes us once more seriously question our real purpose in life.

The cycle probably moves on — but becomes less obvious as we each develop our own nature and maybe discover a personal bias towards a particular direction of thought.

A CYCLE OF FASHION

Consider the sixties occult revival; did it not last for about one generation?

I do not mean that Magic has since been abandoned. Just as we did not abandon technology in the sixties — in fact we had more of it than ever but began to take it for granted — so also there are still more New Age shops and books on Magic available now than there ever were in the sixties and yet we take them for granted. The movement I am trying to isolate is this: between the early sixties and late seventies the public got its kicks from occultism; sensational coverage of parascience, lurid exposes of witches, books on black magic and record covers littered with occult symbolism. For a period of about one generation, Magic had real novelty value and a feeling of real power potential — something it no longer has to any extent.

But if we go back to the end of the nineteenth century we see a similar movement. Theater posters of that era are so rich in occult symbolism (bowls of incense, Egyptian hieroglyphs etc.) that this 'art nouveau' style was actually one of the main sources of inspiration for sixties psychedelia. The turn of the twentieth century was when the Golden Dawn occult society attracted public attention and so many similar orders briefly flourished.

Why this flirtation with the occult? In the late Victorian era of a generation earlier, the theater posters reveal a craze for public scientific demonstrations — theaters putting on shows about the wonders of electricity. It suggests that the Edwardian occult revival could have been a reaction against late Victorian materialism; just as the hippy generation reacted against 50s materialism. Magic following upon Science in the public imagination.

According to my cycle, however, there should have been a Religious phase before the Scientific one. This was very apparent in Victorian times — the Scientific craze referred to the discoveries of Charles Darwin and other fashionable ideas which seemed to knock Religion on the head. But what about the period before the late 40s and 50s materialism? Was the public particularly taken up with Religious thinking? If we admit Fascism and Communism as examples of Religious thought — as I suggest in Chapter 10A — the answer is clearly affirmative.

And before the Thirties there should have been an Artistic craze phase. This is typified by the Roaring Twenties, which saw the popularisation of so many modern art movements, an obsession with 'style', dancing and jazz, and a spate of publicity stunts like long-distance flying records, dancing marathons etc. In this period crude new technologies like radio and cine-matography evolved into art forms.

So the cycle I am sensing runs like this. Towards the beginning of the Nineteenth century there was a craze for spiritualism and mesmerism — a Magical phase. This was followed by an Artistic phase typified by my local town Cheltenham Spa — an elegant town built in a speculative boom for stylish living and health fads. A phase very reminiscent of the 1980s yuppy era and one which similarly ended with a market collapse and Religious revival. People in the mid Victorian period had burned their fingers and returned to church for a while until the Science craze caught on. Then came the previously mentioned Edwardian Magical revival, the Artistic frenzy of the 20s and another market collapse which lead to a search for identity in the twentieth century 'Religions' of politics. Fifties materialism was followed by a sixties Magical revival and another Artistic phase in the 80s. This time the new technologies which matured into Art were computer games and graph-ics. As in the 20s the emphasis was on style, music, and record breaking stunts as well as heady speculation. The 80s stock market crash again paved the way for a sense of seriousness and a new Religious spirit which I detect in the 90s — this time a mixture of pre-millennial religious interest plus a revival of nationalism and football tribalism. Religion has as much shock value in the 90s as Magic had in the late 60s.

So, according to my model, the next generation after the millennium will become once more intoxicated with the wonders of Science. Stuff which is being talked about nowadays but which is really pretty limited and clumsy — like virtual reality, cloning and fractal digital cinematography — these things will really begin to deliver in a few years time. As in the 50s when we became fascinated with the novelty value of Science, we will again begin to believe that Science has an answer for everything — and that will continue until somewhere around 2020 when we will be due for a reaction and another Magical revival. I will then become famous — and too old or dead to care!

A CYCLE OF THOUGHT

According to the last cycle, Richard Dawkins has nothing to fear, because the public isn't really obsessed with Magic, it is rather more taken with the novelty value in millennial Religion — plus its attendant tribalism and nationalism — and it is soon going to rediscover the wonders of Science as we enter a new materialistic post-millennium phase.

He is, however, reacting to something more profound than a public craze cycle. I argue that we are also seeing a slower, more fundamental shift away from Scientific thinking towards Magical thinking, and that this last happened at the end of the Classical era when we moved into what is called the Dark Ages.

According to this cycle, the 500 or so years before Christ were strongly influenced by rational thought which I would characterise as 'Scientific' even though it predates the current meaning of the word. Joseph Needham's Science and Civilisation in China quotes Chinese philosophers of that time pouring scorn on subjects like astrology and lucky numbers using arguments very much like those of modern rationalists. According to S Bochner's *The Role of Mathematics in the Rise of Science* "Purely Mathematically, there is nothing in Newton's Principia that was not familiar to Archimedes, except the notion of the rate of change of a velocity". This is quoted in Jack Linsay's *The Origins of Alchemy In Graeco-Roman Egypt* in which book it is pointed out that Arabic metallurgy did not evolve out of mystical alchemy, but rather the reverse. As in China, the original objective was to imitate gold by chemical means, not to create it — aurifiction not aurifaction.

So the Dark Ages strike me as a time when the rationalist 'Science' of the metallurgists became overlaid with Magical thinking, and neoplatonism took over from the rationalist philosophy of Archimedes and Aristotle. This was followed after about five centuries by a movement more akin to my Artistic thought in an age typified by the troubadours, courtly love and the setting of fairy tales and legends. In the mediaeval period this gave way to Religious thought, which dominated society until around 1500 and the rise of Scientific thought typified by the Enlightenment and reaching its apogee in Victorian times.

In these terms we are now at the end of this era and once more Magical thought is on the ascendent, in the sense that it is beginning to take an intellectual lead in our society — whatever passing phases of fashion might seem to overlay the process as described in the previous novelty cycle.

What is the evidence for a rebirth of Magical thought? This has been discussed at length in my other writings, so I will just list a few examples.

First is the fact that rationalists are feeling very defensive — when you might expect them to be rejoicing in their triumph over the superstition of the past.

Secondly, people are increasingly confusing statistical correlation with Scientific proof. If, for example, some respected medical research institute were to announce a highly significant correlation between coffee and cancer, there would be a public outcry for the banning of coffee — because people would feel that it had been 'Scientifically proven' that this would save lives. In my terms, this would be sympathetic Magical thinking — cancer 'goes with' coffee and so you banish the latter to banish the former — and it would not be Science until a causal link had been identified. This is an example where Magic takes over from Science because Science, through technology, increases change to the point where change happens too fast to be managed by the slow processes of Science.

Thirdly, Science is becoming so complex that communication could break down. Jack Lindsay's book suggests that one factor in changing Arabic metallurgy into mystical alchemy was politically enforced secrecy. Communication of a common body of belief is vital to Science. If you restrict it, Science grows cranky and loses its universality. When I wrote the first edition of this book I saw this happening, and the driving factor was the Cold War. We were hearing of mysterious psychic experiments from behind the Iron Curtain, every bit as weird as some of the Science that went on secretly under the Nazi regime. The situation is now different: we do not have so much military restriction on Science, but there are increasing commercial reasons for secrecy, plus the sheer difficulty of communicating such a vast amount of research. To see what happens when Scientists stop communicating, consider cold fusion: when this was openly debated across the globe a consensus was rapidly reached that it was not repeatable. But now the subject has become taboo, several isolated laboratories around the world are achieving significant results which would have been dismissed as Magic if they had been reported. I believe that, if you isolate a group of Scientists, they evolve away from Scientific consensus and this is a threat which could subvert Science itself.

Fourthly, because it has become traditional to dismiss the reality of Magic, it then means that people can freely practice Magic without admitting it. As in my example in the introduction of the marketing company which is 'really' just invoking the assistance of the god Mercury. If you told them they were practicing Magic they would say "nonsense, this is scientific marketing because it really works and we can prove it" — a definition of 'scientific' which would embrace chanting to make the Sun rise. There are many such examples of Magical practices being accepted loosely under the banner of Science.

Fifthly, Magic can take over when Science loses touch with human need. As in my discussion of alternative medicine in another chapter, any attempt to test remedies by eliminating the role of the placebo effect is as divorced from the human condition as an automobile test conducted with no fuel in the tank in order to 'eliminate extraneous factors'.

Sixthly, some new technologies confound mechanistic analysis. Observation and logic are fundamental to Scientific thinking — if you left an intelligent person alone on a desert island with a clock or steam engine and a few spanners they could eventually discover how it worked, but the same is not true of a silicon chip. Whereas a previous generation felt it necessary to be able to understand how domestic appliances worked, and how to repair them, we increasingly are driven to accept that things either work or they need to be replaced. Learning to accept unexplained phenomena in this way is good training for Magical thinking. Here is an example: as a Fortran programmer in the 1970s, if a program did not work I would return to the source code and analyse it for errors. In the 1990s this is no longer practical — instead I phone a 'help' line and am told there is a 'bug' which means I should try to avoid certain sequences of activity. This is analogous to being told that it is unlucky to walk under ladders. There are two factors here driving the evolution towards Magical thinking: increasing complexity as in the second example, plus commercial pressure which forbids access to the source code, as in the third example.

Seventhly, increasing commercial involvement with pure Science will, according to Magical theory, make it less pure and more Magical. An example: on yesterday's radio discussion I heard a fairly belligerent speaker insist that there was absolutely no evidence that psychological analysis had ever helped cure depression. "That's odd" I thought, "I can immediately think of someone I know who has been helped in this way, and that invalidates that assertion". As if he had read my mind the speaker promptly added "...of course you must not be taken in by anecdotal evidence, I'm talking about hard scientific data". What struck me as curious was this: he was dismissing the evidence of mine own experience, whereas I was more inclined to dismiss the 'hard data' as being less valuable than anecdotal data. Why was this? On reflection I realised that I gave less value to the Scientific research because it was very likely to have been conducted with intent to prove something, whereas mine own observation was nothing more than pure observation. According to Magical theory, the outcome of an act will be influenced by the intent of the actor, so any Scientific experiment or measurement carried out with a desire to prove something will be affected by that desire (Scientists, understandably, would question this assertion). However, increasing commercial funding of universities and research inevitably invokes stronger intent — researchers need to ensure continued funding to support them. According to this theory, the purest Science was that pursued by gentlemen of leisure in the past, or incumbents of wealthy old universities or bloated government bodies who could afford the luxury of pure Scientific exploration without any 'lust for result'. Such conditions are now being eroded — even Oxbridge needs to woo industry, and government itself is trying hard to shed pounds. The long term effect will be to split the consensus of Scientific world-view into rival channels, as has happened with television. Future Scientists will need to choose, for example, whether they accept Scientific truth as defined by Microsoft, or Friends of the Earth, or the nuclear industry, or the French government, or whatever. It will still be called "Science", but it will amount to a choice of belief systems, which is pure Magic.

AN EVEN SLOWER CYCLE

That last cycle amounted to a confirmation of Dawkins' and other rationalists' worst fears — that society is currently moving away from the authority of Scientific thought and is giving increasing credence and authority to Magical thinking; and that the precedent for this change was the coming of the Dark Ages.

The very phrase 'Dark Ages' is enough to send a shiver down rationalist spines, with its sense of a denial of all that enlightenment stands for. But I will now explain why it should be very different this time round, and why today's rationalists will never be quite sure whether they are winning or losing the battle for our minds!

I began by describing a personal cycle I had noticed in mine own education, and then a slower cycle of public crazes. I do not see any link between these two cycles — they are operating at quite different levels and in different contexts. In my case they came together at one point rather nicely, because I was personally getting into Magic at university in the late sixties at the same time as it was catching on as a public craze — and that gave me a lovely feeling of being at the leading edge of contemporary ideas. After a while, however, my personal cycle got out of step and I became disillusioned with that Magical revival.

Next I described another independent cycle, a much slower one, which is concerned with intellectual authority. In this cycle we are at the end of five centuries in which Scientific thought has lead the way, and I suggest that Magical thought is now taking the lead. This cycle will take about two thousand years to repeat.

Now a period of 'two thousand years' brings to mind another Magical theory — that of the astrological aeons. In this theory we are entering the Age of Aquarius after two thousand years of the Age of Pisces and, before that, two thousand years of the Age of Aries.

There is no reason why this cycle has to match up to my scheme, but a link does suggest itself, because the last two thousand years have, on another level, been dominated by Religion — whatever the current intellectual driving force has been. Throughout the Age of Pisces the dominant spirit has been Religious — whether the activity was Magic, Science, Art or Religion, the tendency has been to justify it 'in God's name'. Even Scientists have until recently been wary of accusations that they are undermining Religious authority or acting against divine will. The dominant Artistic heritage of the age has been Religious, traditional Magical texts are heavily overlaid with Religious imagery and language, and the majority of wars have been fought on Religious/political grounds.

Compare that spirit with the previous, classical era when the most famous (Trojan) war was fought over a beautiful woman! Replace the dominance of Religion with a dominance of Art and culture and you get much more the feeling of the previous age of Aries (there is even a sense that an earlier pre-classical era was dominated by nations with the most powerful Magic).

In this cycle, then, the new age of Aquarius will be dominated by the Scientific spirit. Guernica was perhaps a turning point — a battle fought ostensibly on idealistic grounds but actually so the Germans could test their bombs. Tomorrow's wars will be an excuse to try out military hardware to justify the billions of public money spent upon it. So no matter how Arty, Magical or Religious we are being, it will all tend to be done in the name of Science.

As I suggested in the first edition of this book, we won't hear so much about 'a return to Magical thinking' as about 'the birth of the soft Sciences', of 'a new holistic Science', 'feminine Science' and so on (and since that edition some of these phrases have actually been used). As in my introductory example of the marketing agency, people will insist that they are being very Scientific even when blatantly practicing Magic. The whole New Age phenomenon reflects this contradiction between the two cycles — people opting for phrases like 'quantum consciousness' and shying away from the more concise traditional Magical terminology.

Let us return to an early example from this chapter, the talk by Richard Dawkins at the 1998 Cheltenham Festival. He was announcing a new book called *Unweaving the Rainbow* which took its title from a conversation between some romantic poets who cursed Newton for having destroyed the beauty of the rainbow through his explanation of the properties of light. Dawkins felt sad, yet sympathetic to this attitude, and he set out to redress the balance by showing the many ways in which Science can invoke wonderment, awe and aesthetic pleasure. The result was a wonderful presentation by a man appointed to be a public spokesman for Science — but was it Scientific?

I would say that the task Dawkins had set himself was this: to change the public perception of Science. 'Changing perceptions', however is not a Scientific but a Magical process in my usage. In a world defined in terms of truth and falsehood, Science may set out to *clarify* perceptions, but not to *change* them. A more truly Scientific response to those romantic poets would be to admit that a certain sense of awe might have been destroyed by the Newtonian analysis of the rainbow, but to insist that the awe was a primitive emotional reaction and, in its place, we now had a superior understanding which was worth far more because Truth has its own higher Beauty... or something along those lines.

I enjoyed Dawkins' talk because I felt he was attempting a Magical transformation of Science into something more acceptable to changing tastes. It was quite good Magic, and yet it would not now be admitted as such, for his official role is something to do with educating the public about Science.

My role is to educate the public about Magic, but it will probably not be officially recognised in the Age of Aquarius when I would do better to invent snappy New Age pseudo-scientific terminology for my thesis rather than present it in traditional magical terminology!

WHY THESE CYCLES?

Remember, this is an example of a Magical theory. It relies upon verification and not falsification. When I describe the two thousand years before Christ as being dominated by the Artistic spirit, the clever reader is not the one who looks for counter-evidence, but the one who can sense the truth in that statement. In this way the reader gives value to the theory and this allows it to become powerful and useful — with predictive and explanatory ability. The trick then is not to forget that it is just a Magical theory — even if it seems to explain everything, you should resist the Religious or Scientific temptation to equate it with 'truth'.

As a Magical theory it does not need to have a single cause or reason behind it — a cycle is just a cycle. But it is naturally human to look for some underlying cause.

In the case of the novelty cycle, I recall a feeling in the early sixties that 'there must be something more' than the materialism if the fifties. Rationalist explanations for everything from falling in love to the Religious instinct were no longer liberating us from dogmatic Religious traditions, instead they began to sound just as 'smart ass' and smug as the old Religious tenets. On the other hand, Magic was such an outdated idea that it had revolutionary appeal. Turning to Magic had the feeling of a 'turning inward', away from the crass surface qualities of materialism to find something 'deeper' within.

This turning away from materialism was not a physical act. On the contrary, people bought more radios, televisions, cars and gadgets than ever before — maybe that was why these marvels of technology lost their novelty appeal and became essentials rather than luxuries.

Similarly, in the eighties, people did not abandon the tarot cards, astrological readings and amulets of the Magical revival. On the contrary, books on 'mind, body and spirit' became so common as to lose their novelty value to designer labels and fashion foods.

During the nineties, I sensed that people were growing bored with 'the inner quest'. It was as if they had done so many inner child workshops and tarot readings that they yearned for something bigger than their own over-explored psyches. They began to look outward and wanted to be part of or aligned with something bigger, a truth which lay 'out there' — and that was a driver towards a revival of Religious thinking. It manifests itself as a search for some absolute standard, some higher power, or a nation or at least a team or tribal affiliation which is hoped to be greater than the sum of its parts. Even the current fascination with the paranormal and ufos has more to do with a Religious quest than Magical practice.

Why should we next turn back to Science? I anticipate it will be because millennial fever will have abated and technology will begin to deliver some of the miracles of information technology and genetic engineering now being promised.

Another possibility is to look for some astrological correlate, though there is no reason why it should exist. The nearest I can see is that Neptune in air signs go with Science as fashion — maybe through idealising reason; Neptune in water idealises feeling and Magic; Neptune in fire idealises creativity so Art is fashion; while Neptune in earth does not so much idealise matter as erode materialism and initiate a search for new boundaries in nationalism, tribalism and Religion.

That fashion cycle is a fairly superficial cycle, and it hardly justifies a major shift in humanity's ideas. Looking at the bigger picture I can see how the tendency of Religion is to evolve towards monotheism. This leads to a crisis, because a monotheistic Religion eventually comes up against the material world. The physical world can happily coexist with a pantheon of nature spirits, but how can it be allowed to exist when there is only one reality — and that is God? Ultimately this can be resolved by making the material universe itself into God — ie by concluding that matter is the only reality, and that the proper study of it is Science. Thus Religion will inevitably give way to Science. Another theory is that a Religious society, with its strong traditions, tends to be a stable society — and stability is a condition suitable for the spread of knowledge and therefore a fertile basis for the rise of Science.

Science, on the other hand, encourages change. It leads to new technologies and these impose accelerating change on society. The problem here is that Scientific thought is too slow to cope with the speed of change which arises — people begin to need immediate solutions as in my example of banning some new chemical or process because it correlates statistically with cancer. People need recourse to Magic to cope with the changes brought about by Science. What is more, the expansion of Science becomes so rapid that the subject begins to fragment — and this goes against the need for free communication of concepts. Once Science fragments into discrete groups who no longer share information, as it did at the end of the classical era, then it grows cranky and... er, interesting. So Science will eventually give way to Magic.

Magic begins with the desire to control a turbulent world but, as anyone who has studied it eventually discovers, it evolves towards transformation of experience. Instead of trying to control the world's finances, experienced Magicians usually put more effort into transcending them. Magical groups end up doing more rituals to celebrate Nature than to control Her. Thus Magic tends to evolve into Art, ritual into drama.

Art, in turn, seems to evolve from popular tribal celebration towards a more exclusive and individual voyage of discovery — and that sets the scene for a personal Religious experience or conversion, and the cycle begins again.

It is as if the four faculties I introduced — logic, observation, feeling and intuition — co-existed in a cyclic hierarchy like the childrens' game of 'paper, scissors, stone' where scissors cut paper, stone sharpens scissors and paper wraps stone.

First imagine a situation dominated by intuition — for example a millennial cult where everyone is in thrall of the preachings channelled by the cult leader. What is the one person who cannot be tolerated in such a cult? It is the rational enquirer who gently points out that — however convincing the leader's arguments for the end of the world — he is not the first person who has made a similar case and been proven wrong. Such a person cannot be tolerated because logic is the one faculty stronger than intuition.

Now imagine a situation dominated by logic — maybe an academic think tank addressing economic problems. Fact is the nemesis of such a mindset — however brilliant and flawless the logical arguments put forward, they will be defeated by events which contradict their predictions because observation is the only faculty stronger than logic. If you are in a situation dominated by someone who can always win verbal arguments, then it is no good appealing to feeling judgements or an intuitive sense that he is wrong. Instead you must say "that is very interesting, so you should be able to produce some real-world figures to back up your case and even make some verifiable predictions for tomorrow's results. Can you?".

I was once explaining this dominance of observation over logic to someone and they squashed my argument by saying "yes, but there are good statistics and bad statistics, of course." The reason I was squashed was that, by ascribing the words 'good' and 'bad' to what should be objective results, my companion had demonstrated the next relationship — that the only faculty stronger than observation is feeling.

44

On the other hand, when a situation is dominated by feeling it is as useless to try to resolve it with facts as it is to use logic — because the only faculty stronger than feeling is intuition. Going back to our millennial cult — many such cults begin with a group of high-minded people with strong feelings for what is decent and good and looking for ways to help the world. Then one charismatic leader has an intuitive flash or message from god, and it is accepted by the members even when it leads them away from their original principles towards paranoia and cruelty. The leader's intuition eventually overwhelms those finer sensibilities because intuition is the only faculty stronger than feeling.

So I have suggested that maybe the cycle of thought has its roots in a circular hierarchy of our mental faculties. One cycle driving another — so many Magical theories are cyclical. Maybe our species has evolved in this way because such an arrangement fosters continuous change and, being circular, endless change. Because humanity cannot sit still, it has to grow.

Or maybe I have simply projected my own inner experience onto history!

THE LEGACY OF CYCLES

A curious by-product of these cycles is that each way of thinking tends to inherit a burden from its predecessor. This burden is more or less unconscious and tends to muddy the waters of my comparatively neat model.

Consider Science, for example. According to my definition it should be securely founded on reason and observation with no need for dogmatism. Indeed, this objective, open-mindedness would be strongly claimed by Scientists themselves. However, Scientific thinkers are all too often highly dogmatic, especially when debating spiritual topics when phrases like 'mumbo jumbo' and 'New Age nonsense' spring almost automatically from their lips. This unconscious dogmatism is Science's legacy from Religious thought: in the Religion sector faith is a virtue to which one aspires, in the Science sector it has become an unconscious habit one seeks to transcend.

Magic, in turn, inherits unconscious skepticism from Science. Just as the 'open minded' Scientist is deep down a total believer in material reality, so also the 'gullible' Magician deep down does not really believe in anything. When astrologers, for example, get together one of the commonest conversational gambits is "last week I had Saturn pass over my Mercury and — it's absolutely incredible — my car broke down three days running!". Ritual magicians can be heard saying "we did this healing rite and — it's absolutely incredible — next time he went to the doctor there was no sign of the tumour". Can you imagine a group of chemists getting together and saying "I put this litmus paper into the acid and — it's absolutely incredible — it changed colour"?

SSOTBME - AN ESSAY ON MAGIC - REVISED

As I explained in my second volume of essays — Blast Your Way To Megabuck$ With My SECRET Sex-Power Formula — what so many un-evolved Magical thinkers are trying to do is to convince themselves of the reality of a Magic which, deep down, they do not believe can really exist. In the Science sector an open, skeptical mind is a virtue that one aspires to, in the Magic sector it is an inner emptiness one seeks to fill with meaning.

Insofar as practical Magic demands an ability to switch beliefs at will, an underlying skepticism is not a bad thing. But it can be just as corrosive as the Scientist's dogmatism, and it really shows when Scientists and Magicians get into argument. Typically the Scientist is the first to succumb: as soon as the conversation moves to 'other realities' the Scientist is liable to smell a subversive Magical rat and lapse into mindless phrases like "utter poppycock". At this stage the Magicians usually have the intellectual high ground as they are typically out-Sciencing the Scientist by asking whether the evidence has been considered and so on. However they all too often lose this advantage and themselves lapse into haranguing the Scientist whose scornful dogmatism echoes their own hidden fear that Magic is indeed a load of deluded crap! Of course, both sides would reject my explanation totally and insist that their arguments were based entirely on fact.

I'm not so sure about the burden that Art inherits from Magic, but suspect that it could be a sense of 'meaning'. It always struck me as a bit odd how people can be irritated by modern art because they do not 'understand it', and how they can feel much happier when offered some bogus 'explanation' — eg "Mondrian's paintings are made up of a grid of straight black lines symbolising the order and rules of modern civilisation, dividing areas of bright colour which represent the human passions being restrained by these rules". I used to think that the demand for explanation was a product of our Scientific culture, but maybe it is a legacy from Magic. A poet once told me that it was wrong to think of a symbol as a sort of telephone number connecting one to an idea, and I was surprised because that is exactly what it is in Magical usage. There is, for example, a sort of tick symbol extant in our culture which is used to call up Nike, the goddess of victory — you see advertisements with sweaty athletes and some slogan like 'make history or be it' and this little tick inserted as the one element to give the arbitrary picture some meaning. Surely that is Magic, not Art.

A Magical image — like an alchemical illustration or a tarot card — is a picture where every element is deliberately built into the picture for its symbolic associations. I am sure that most Artists would scorn such an approach: indeed those, like Salvador Dali, who approximate to it receive little critical acclaim for such imagery. True Art, we are told, needs no such artificial crutches, and yet how many Artists can claim never to have felt comforted or even justified by those who read 'meaning' into their work? In

46

the Magic sector meaning is a precious thing, a pointer towards wholeness, while in the Art sector meaning has become a tangle of associations that one seeks to cut away to reveal life in its pure essence.

I am equally unqualified to judge what is the unconscious burden Religion inherits from Art, but my guess is that it is glamour. The Southern baptist turns scornfully away from the theater of popish robes and smells, only to create their own rock 'n roll glamour in turn. Even the most extreme puritanism of the Shakers comes across to us as 'high style'.

COMPASS, NOT CLASSIFICATION

I insist that the four-fold diagram is a compass of directions and not a definer of categories, and yet I use the terms Magic, Science, Art and Religion as if they were four distinct disciplines.

Sorry.

It's the easy way to write — just like it's easy to say I live "in the South West". But I am allowed to talk about The South etc, because people understand my double use of the word as a direction and a temporary definition of place.

Here the usage is less familiar, so I decide to explain once again that Magical theories tend to be infinitely translatable in the way a compass is. The same compass can be used to divide the globe into four cultures, Britain into four regions, Gloucester into four quarters or a house into four wings. So also the thought-compass of this book can be focussed down to analyse ever narrower activities.

If I take advertising as an example of human activity, it should be no surprise to learn that, from where I stand, I consider it to be a form of Magic. Other people consider it to be art or science, maybe. But the fact that I consider it to be Magic does not force me to deny that advertising can dress itself in the imagery of Art, Science or Religion. It less often uses Magical imagery except for specific niche markets, or at times like the sixties and seventies when Magic was fashion — why is this? I guess that advertising creatives would describe Magical imagery as 'too cheesy' and, if so, I would ask them to qualify the 'too'. Because I suspect that the people who would be embarrassed would not be the public but rather the advertising industry itself. It shies away from Magical imagery because it would rather not face the possibility that it is a branch of Magic!

Anyway, let us apply the compass within advertising and recognise that it has its 'Scientific' quarter — a tradition for presenting the technical benefits of certain sorts of products. So here are four off-the-cuff fictitious advertising slogans for toothpaste.

Dukesodent — a better toothpaste. Your money back if you don't agree.

Dukesodent — the only toothpaste endorsed by the British Dental Association.

Dukesodent — the only toothpaste featuring ionisation-enhancing free radical plaque inhibition agents.

Dukesodent — the hi-tech toothpaste for the hi-tech generation.

All four slogans lean towards the Science side of advertising, in my terms, and yet I can still draw a distinction between them with my four directions.

Only the first is specifically Scientific in my terms, because it appeals primarily to observation (try it yourself) and logic (they couldn't offer money back unless it was reasonably good).

The second has every bit as much logical appeal — it must be pretty good for BDA approval. But it makes little appeal to observation, because only a small minority of people have enough direct experience to know about the BDA and its mechanisms for product endorsement, and the advertisement is not directed towards that niche. For the general public the value of BDA approval is based primarily upon intuitive acceptance of their priestly authority in dental matters — a Religious appeal.

Compare the third, the one with the most blatant Scientific imagery. Again, for a small niche market of dental technicians this could (if the words made sense) have genuine Scientific appeal, but for the general public it is pure Magic — touching lightly on personal experience of plaque and helpful Scientific additives, but relying far more on good feelings for impressive words than any logical or causal understanding.

The fourth is purely a style statement — Art in my terms.

Thus demonstrating, I trust, that this theory is not a statement about absolute categories but simply an indicator of relative positioning. Each quadrant contains all four directions — just as every astrological sign contains the entire zodiac, and every sphere of the Cabalistic tree of life contains the whole tree.

PLAYING THE COMPASS

It strikes me that you could play with this cycle as a conversational gambit in the presence of anyone who is strongly polarised towards one of my four directions of thought.

This is how you do it. If you want to irritate the speaker, question his ideas from the perspective of the previous quadrant. To offend or disturb, use the opposite quadrant. To intrigue and stimulate, use the following quadrant.

So, if speaking to a rationalist or Scientist, you can irritate with Religious-style statements such as "certainly we can clone humans, but the real question is *should* we clone humans?". You can disturb them with Artistic statements such as "but wouldn't you agree that the Moon Project has destroyed much of the awe and mystery of that heavenly body?". Or you can stimulate with Magical questions such as "if I want to cure depression is it more effective to approach it as a psychological condition, or as a chemical condition?" (ie how do I adjust my perceptions to increase the chance of success).

To irritate a Religious mind put the Artistic questions about the aesthetics of creation "how can a supposedly good God have created a world where the holocaust is allowed to happen?". To disturb or offend, ask such Magical questions as "does Israeli military success in the Middle East signify that Jehovah is a more credible deity than Allah?" To stimulate debate apply the logic and observation of Science and ask "if you really want to spread your message, shouldn't you be preaching via the mass media rather than in cold churches?"

To irritate the Artist ask the Magical question "what does this picture mean?". To disturb, put the Scientific viewpoint "if you want a public wouldn't it be better to work with television rather than oil paints?" To stimulate, try the Religious tack and discuss the ethical or political implications of their work.

To irritate a Magician put the Scientific question "but can you be absolutely sure that the cure wasn't just coincidence?". To disturb, put such Religious moral questions as "what gives you the right to intervene in another person's state of health?". To stimulate, make some suggestions about the aesthetics or dramatic format of a ritual.

Of course, the real communicative value of this idea is not so much how to use it to disturb or offend, but rather what sort of dialogue to avoid if you wish to foster genuine communication with other minds.

CONCLUSION

In this chapter the 'compass of thought' was put to use, exploring changes in society. I looked at the feeling among some rationalists that we are slipping back into atavistic, superstitious thought patterns, and suggested that this could not be possible unless such ways of thinking offered some advantage over rationalism.

Exploring my own development I discerned a cycle in which Science did indeed pave the way to Magic, and it was indeed an advance in my thinking. Seen in terms of this cycle, the immediate media frenzy is not so much about Magic as Religion — today's trendy truth lies 'out there' rather than 'within' — and Science is poised to make a big comeback.

On a more serious level, however, Scientific rationalism is eroding on many fronts and we are indeed entering the equivalent of a 'dark ages', but I do not believe it will be quite so dark as the last one because Scientific principles have now got too strong a hold. Everything, however irrational, will be done 'in the name of Science' and the ideas in this book will be largely ignored until someone has the wit to re-phrase them in suitably pseudo-scientific New Age terminology.

Finally, just in case the picture is getting too neat, I pointed out that in practice each way of thought tends, in practice to carry a burden from its predecessor in the cycle. In don't think that bit will win many friends, but it could help sort out a few bitter arguments.

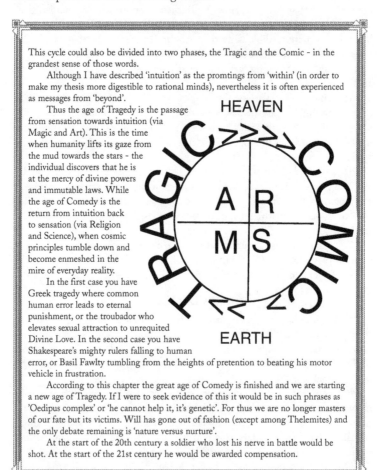

This cycle could also be divided into two phases, the Tragic and the Comic - in the grandest sense of those words.

Although I have described 'intuition' as the promtings from 'within' (in order to make my thesis more digestible to rational minds), nevertheless it is often experienced as messages from 'beyond'.

Thus the age of Tragedy is the passage from sensation towards intuition (via Magic and Art). This is the time when humanity lifts its gaze from the mud towards the stars - the individual discovers that he is at the mercy of divine powers and immutable laws. While the age of Comedy is the return from intuition back to sensation (via Religion and Science), when cosmic principles tumble down and become enmeshed in the mire of everyday reality.

In the first case you have Greek tragedy where common human error leads to eternal punishment, or the troubador who elevates sexual attraction to unrequited Divine Love. In the second case you have Shakespeare's mighty rulers falling to human error, or Basil Fawlty tumbling from the heights of pretention to beating his motor vehicle in frustration.

According to this chapter the great age of Comedy is finished and we are starting a new age of Tragedy. If I were to seek evidence of this it would be in such phrases as 'Oedipus complex' or 'he cannot help it, it's genetic'. For thus we are no longer masters of our fate but its victims. Will has gone out of fashion (except among Thelemites) and the only debate remaining is 'nature versus nurture'.

At the start of the 20th century a soldier who lost his nerve in battle would be shot. At the start of the 21st century he would be awarded compensation.

50

CHAPTER FOUR
"Sex secrets of the black magicians exposed"

It is hoped that anyone who has any practical experience of Magic will by now agree that this essay is indeed about magic. However, experience suggests that some readers will feel that I have evaded the real subject by omitting to mention screaming virgins, sacrificed goats and chalices of warm blood.

Though I would be the last to deny the Magical importance of such things, yet I insist that their importance is more peripheral than basic. For all the books on Magic which provide lurid details of bloody sabbats, there are many of the more practical step-by-step introductions which go no further than accounts of breathing exercises and meditations. And yet both types of book are about Magic.

Books with titles like 'Sex Secrets of the Black Magicians Exposed' are the equivalent in scope to books with titles like 'The Wonderland of Science'. The image of the black robed Magician is no more and no less essential than the image of the Scientist in a white lab coat. If one's only experience of Science was through the children's books with pictures of cyclotrons, radio telescopes and lasers, then a basic chemistry course at high school would seem a terrible let-down. It would be hard to believe that it had anything to do with Science as one had learnt to understand the word. Those 'boring' meditation books are just the equivalent of a Teach Yourself Chemistry text.

When you consider that the transition from basic physics to cyclotrons extends over many years of study via high school, university and research degrees, then it will seem less than reasonable to expect any one book to bridge satisfactorily the gap between thinking about thinking and screaming virgins, least of all in a short essay such as this. All that can be done is to explain why I consider that the importance of sacrificed goats has been exaggerated.

Without going into great details as to what I 'really believe', it can be argued that, in some sense at least, the Devil was a creation of the Church. Firstly, as one Religion replaces another, it is desirable to discredit the old Gods; and if there is nothing but Good in your scheme, it is hard to explain where the old Gods went wrong. Therefore, it was desirable to have a Devil so that the Christians could explain how the old God was in fact a smooth-tongued baddy who hoodwinked his followers.

But the Devil's usefulness does not end there. When Religious thought holds authority, the reason and intuition of the Religious leaders are all-powerful. So error and failure were rejected or denied and, in analogy with the personal 'shadow' of the analytical psychologists, such debris collected around the symbol of the Devil, having nowhere else to go. The Devil was also very necessary to the feeble human who found the word of the Lord was insufficient to keep him moving on the paths of righteousness, and who needed the hot breath of brimstone over his shoulder to drive him forward.

Through accumulating all the rejections of authority, this symbol gained power in men's minds and so unfortunately it gained fascination. The symbol which started as a sort of rubbish dump had grown more exciting and alluring than Christianity itself. The Devil was indeed a Magical being. In opposition to the reason and intuition of the Religious leaders, the Devil was a creature of feeling and of observation (in the sense that his world was the world of flesh and sensual excitement).

Just as a Religion-dominated society finds it necessary to create a world of un-God, so it seems a Science-dominated society needs a world of un-Truth in order to outline its ideals more clearly.

When presenting to a Scientist arguments in favour of Magical practice in terms of the microcosm — ie the operator's own mind, the retort is often on the lines of "Yes, but that's very different from saying that some sort of gaseous intelligence or 'spirit' is going to come wafting from the planet Venus in answer to your prayer." The idea seems to be that such 'inner world' arguments are all very clever and 'modern', but they are far removed from 'real' magic, ie the delusions of past centuries when people were prepared to believe in anything.

This is far from being the case. Anyone who studies early Magical texts — for example, those by Ficino or Agrippa — and who makes the slightest effort to allow for the way that the use of words might have altered and evolved, can only be surprised at how sensible the discussion was. Even in mediaeval texts, we find that the likelihood of angels and demons being part of the man's own mind was realised and allowed for. What we do not find is the implicit Scientific deduction that being part of our own minds means that they 'don't exist'. True, some ludicrous and superstitious theories of Magic will be met, particularly when forming part of Religious propaganda, but for that matter it is still possible in this age to find some very peculiar ideas being defended in an apparently Scientific manner.

Remember, if your research into old texts uncovers only mumbo-jumbo, before dismissing it ask yourself: a) is the example totally free of Religious propaganda influence? b) could it be an over-credulous interpretation of what might have been a sensible earlier text? and c) does the example suffer from translation, or a shift with time in the significance of the words used? An old word meaning 'breath', for example, is likely to have meant something experiential, yet more than just a lungful of nitrogen and carbon dioxide.

So where did the idea of an intelligent 'gas' from Venus arise? Certainly such ideas have developed in the same way as the Devil developed: they are usually used by the Scientific mind in an attempt to explain more clearly what it is that it does not believe in. Scientists rejoiced in telling us that the sky was not a solid lid with heaven above it, but who ever believed it was? You have to go an awful long way back to find intelligent discussion of such an idea — unless you are yourself gullible enough to mistake myths for the rational beliefs of the age. For that matter, even in this century children have been told that stars are the holes in the floor of heaven.

At a more subtle level, we find that the Scientist still creates an impossible view of Magic in order that he may reject it. He will quote yesterday's newspaper horoscope guide and announce that its errors show there to be 'nothing in' astrology. It does not seem to occur to him that the announcement that "Gemini will receive important news this morning . ." is from a truly astrological viewpoint merely the equivalent of the fashion prediction that "everybody will be wearing pastel colours this season." Similarly, he will ask the advice of a consultant astrologer, and when the astrologer asks: "Have you ever suffered any separation from your parents?", the Scientist will answer: "I'm not going to tell you anything. Let's see how good an astrologer you really are." Would the Scientist do the same to his doctor? When complaining about backache and the doctor asks: "Have you ever had an injury in this area?", would the Scientist answer: "I'm not going to tell you. Let's see how good a doctor you are." I have heard more than one conjuror debunking clairvoyance because they were able to swot up on 'cold reading' techniques and fool the public that they were using clairvoyance — sometimes even giving identical readings to two different members of the public in front of hidden video cameras. Does this 'disprove' clairvoyance? If so, what about those fraudsters who have successfully mimicked doctors or surgeons and got away with it — does that disprove medical science?

In fact the Scientist is demanding that astrology or clairvoyance, a subject which has been neglected and left to be the hobby of eccentrics for over a century, should be more accurate and reliable than medicine — where practitioners have to study intensively for years and be examined to the highest standards. Once again the Scientist needs to create the impossible in order to refute it.

Just as in Religious times, we were warned of man's tendency to 'follow weakly in the ways of the Devil', nowadays we are taught that the mechanism of our brain is imperfect as a computer, and so the brain is susceptible to illusion and group hysteria. Instead of original sin, we have mechanical imperfection, instead of evil, we have illusion or fraud. But just as the old anti-moral ideas collected around and lent fascination to the Devil, so do the new anti-truth ideas gather and create a fascinating world of hysteria, fantasy and fraud. This magic un-truth world seduces the Scientific mind, as did the Devil seduce the Religious. The Scientific thinker wants un-truth and reacts irrationally when disappointed of it: Uri Geller is despised because he fails to bend any spoon under any condition that the Scientist imposes.

We still use the word 'magic' to describe this world of un-truth, but I would argue that it is a world closer to my use of the word 'Art', For Art, a combination of feeling and intuition, is the polar opposite of Science's logic and observation.

The Scientist, using the word 'magic' in this way, would not like my suggestion that observation is basic to Magic. For him, magic is the ultimate escape from his idea of the world: magic is about fantasy, dream worlds, uncontrolled drug experiences and Dadaist-type happenings. But this is a mistaken idea.

True, the Magician does work in regions which would be described by the Scientist as fantasy worlds: but he is not a Magician unless he is trying to bring about some change in himself or his environment in the process. A Dadaist 'happening' is Magic if it is performed in order to 'shatter middle class morality', to 'change our awareness of the meaning of art', or to 'make money'. If on the other hand, it is done for its own sake, or as a despairing or spontaneous act, then it is Art. Similarly, the controlled drug experience with some such aim as 'self knowledge' or 'the invocation of genius' is Magic whereas a sociable freak-out is probably not.

I do not want to give the impression of belittling Art — it is not that Artistic thought is chaotic and aimless, but rather that, like Religion, it has motives which are more subtle than the 'in order to' motives of Magic and Science.

So a popular idea of Magic as a thrilling bat and virgin infested escape from the boring world of Science's creation is in fact tangential to real Magic: the Scientific mind has created an enemy more exciting than Science itself. Books on Magic which fail to present the bizarre and sinister are not therefore attempts to whitewash the subject, but are probably genuine books on elementary Magic.

On the other hand, this bizarre world of goats and blood is far from being irrelevant to Magic. It is a world which has power over some minds — all the more so for being rejected as 'unreal' by Science. For that reason alone it is a 'real' world in terms of Magic, and so could be used. A Magician wanting to generate maximum psychic tension in his ritual does well to introduce these elements provided that he is able to control them: for even if they prove to be the gothick recreation of an over-materialistic Victorian age, they have got sufficient hold upon our imagination to be useful. As for the sexual element: in a sense sex is Magical by definition, but there are also more subtle ways of employing sex than the sado-masochistic orgies which are popularly associated with the subject of Magic.

Finally it should be noted how the power of this fantasy world of untruth qualifies the conclusion of my last chapter — that Religion, Art, Magic and Science were independent and would therefore find nothing, or come to no conclusion, in attempting to investigate each other in their own terms. This was a description of the ideal state of these elements of thought, and they are seldom found in such a pure state, least of all when one is the dominant system.

In a previous age, a Religious investigation of Magic, Art or Science would in fact reach definite conclusions: everywhere it would find evil, seduction or heresy respectively. Similarly in our own age, it would be surprising if a Scientific investigation actually came to no conclusions about Magic. Such cautious or evasive days are long past. Almost certainly we would now expect the conclusion to contain the elements 'fraud', 'illusion' or 'self deception while under the influence of a dominant personality', all elements projecting from the dustbin world of un-truth.

Is this a sneer at so-called Scientific objectivity? Seen from a Scientific viewpoint, it might seem objectionable to suggest that man is still deceiving himself as he used to in the past. But the very words 'deceiving himself' come from the Scientist's dustbin world. I am as much making a plea that we should be more sympathetic towards the Religious dogmatists of old. The viewpoint is Magical; the respective 'moralities' of Religion and Science cannot be applied.

In fact a Scientific investigation which came to any conclusion in favour of Magic would be as disturbing to me as to other Scientists.

CHAPTER 4A
Demons and sacrifices

For a fuller exploration of the demonic, the fascination of the shadow side and the nature of magical pacts with demons, see my third volume of essays *What I Did In My Holidays*.

See also the second volume of essays — Blast Your Way To Megabuck$ With My SECRET Sex-Power Formula — for the title essay includes an exploration of the myth of Dionysus as a battle between control and ecstacy. It points out that the desire to control has a way of invoking an opposite reaction — as in mind-control cults which so often turn paranoid. Just as the arrival of Dionysus seemed to coincide with the apogee of Greek civilisation and social stability, so also, in present times, just as government gains the most sophisticated technology for controlling the people, precisely then does there arise a Dionysian madness in the population to defy that control. In those cases where government does triumph over the people — eg in Nazi Germany, China and the Soviet Union — then the madness will tend to infect government itself.

I see this argument as qualifying the remarks in the last chapter about Science creating a devil more exciting than itself. I was very much aware of the extent to which the transition of fashion away from Science towards Magic in the sixties was a Dionysian reaction against the know-all smugness of Scientific opinion. I would add this to my list — in Chapter 3A — of reasons why Science gives way to Magic.

Some people find it hard to swallow my use of the words 'devil', 'demon', 'angel' to describe what they see as simply complex processes. When I describe, say, an inferiority complex as a personal demon, or I personify the weather or nature as a god, or when I speak of 'the media' as if it was a living entity — is this no more than a throw-back to primitive animism? Or is it simply a confusion of everyday processes with 'real' demons?

The real question is this: what makes the human brain so much more complex than the brain of other apes? Has all this processing power evolved to handle tools? or is the complexity required to handle social relationships?

Personally, I believe that no mechanical process is more complex than our fellow human beings, and that the human brain has developed first and foremost because of social pressure from other humans. So that when we address a complex problem — eg the weather, market forces, a misbehaving car or a crowd — then greater brain power is available if we anthropomorphise the problem.

The 'rational' objection to this is that, if we know that it is not a person, then we are setting off on a wrong initial assumption. But I suggest this is not a problem, because mechanistic explanations are not a separate category from psychological ones, they are merely a subset. Most human behaviour can eventually be resolved into mechanical reactions, but nevertheless most inter-personal problems are more rapidly solved if you treat the other person as a human being rather than a complex mechanism.

If, for example, my car is an erratic starter on exactly the days when I am in the greatest hurry, then it might prove better to ask "how does it know I am in a hurry" than to insist that "it is only a car and cannot possibly know I am in a hurry". The former question might lead more quickly to the discovery of a loose contact which is disturbed when I slam the door harder — a rational, mechanical explanation and yet one reached more efficiently by using the full animistic potential of the human brain.

A more realistic example is to consider what happened recently when the so-called 'hedge funds' had to be bailed out by the banks. They based their operation upon equations appropriate to the random movements of the stock market, and they were doing exceptionally well until the Asian crisis upset the market equilibrium. Suddenly they were performing worse than the 'intuitive' share dealers. My interpretation of this was that a steady-state financial market is akin to a sleeping brain, and that it only wakes up in response to crisis. While it is 'asleep' its behaviour averages towards random-ness and can be handled by the mathematics of random processes; but when it wakes up it is reacting and no longer random, so the equations no longer apply and the successful dealers are those who lay aside their formulae and use skills more like human counselling or martial arts to 'psychoanalyse' the markets.

In these terms the Magical technique of personifying complexes, institutions and problems can be seen as a powerful approach. It uses the greater part of the brain where a strictly Scientific approach uses only the subset of reasoning that is applicable to linear, mechanistic phenomena.

I am not arguing now that Science is inferior to Magic — it is more a question of breadth versus depth, or parallel versus linear processing. When I discuss the Media, say, as if it was a god which does not act altogether in our interests, I am using the full breadth of my mental capabilities to analyse and predict media reactions. If instead I insist that 'there is no such entity as "the Media"' and I proceed to analyse it as a assemblage of individual bits then I am using only my rational function, but I may well be using that in greater depth. What I do wish to claim is that Magical thought is not simply a more primitive form of Science.

The books mentioned at the beginning of this chapter do not expand much on the subject of animal sacrifices, as I recall — and I am buggered if I am going to read the bloody things right now just to see if I recall rightly. So I add a few words here.

Blood sacrifice plays a very minor role in modern Magic — there is nothing even remotely approaching the massive global slaughter of turkeys for the Christmas ritual, or other world religious sacrifices. Indeed, the current fusion of Paganism and Magic means that most Magicians feel very close to the animal world and actively oppose animal sacrifice to the point of being strictly vegetarian. So I can only quote from mine own experience.

My first animal sacrifice was not a conscious choice, it was largely driven by circumstances. It happened when I was driving at high speed down a country lane on my way to visit a new client for the first time. I was in a hurry because it was vital that I arrived in good time and made a good impression. But I hit a bird at speed and left it dead upon the road. In this narrow lane at rush hour it would have been dangerous to have stopped and walked back, and I did not have time to park and attend to the bird's remains, so I simply drove on — feeling bad. This bad feeling was not conducive to a good working day, so I asked myself if there was any meaning in the bird's death — why had it died? The answer was that it had died because I was driving fast intent upon doing well for my new client. I therefore decided to accept responsibility for the death of the bird and to honour its death — and therefore its life — by making an exceptional conscious effort in my day's work. The work I did that day would be my very best as a tribute to the bird I had sacrificed for it. Many years on that day's new client is still my best client.

Some people might argue that the role of circumstance in that first example disqualified it for the term 'ritual sacrifice' — the death had simply happened and was only later made sacred and Magical. So I give another example where I actually chose to kill — changing a few details because I do not think the reader has the right to know much about me, but it remains true in its essence.

In the streets of Cheltenham I saw what I thought was a polythene bag flipping about in the wind — only there was no wind. Driving closer I saw it was a kitten in mortal agony, its pale fur totally sodden and slimy from leaping and writhing in the wet gutter, one eyeball hanging out of its battered head. It must have been wounded by a car and been squandering its remaining eight lives for quite a while to have got into such a mess. I felt sick, but too squeamish and shocked to attempt to catch this leaping apparition and try to locate a vet, so I decided to take its life as a ritual sacrifice. The kitten's evident suffering left no time to decide a useful intent as would normally be required of a Magical act, so I resolved to make a ritual sacrifice in its purest form and then direct the energy towards manifestation afterwards. I chose a

59

cowardly technique of running over the kitten several times to ensure thorough death and then I picked the remains up with an old carrier bag and placed it in a bin as a marginally more dignified resting place than the road would have been.

Now I had the problem of completing the ritual, because there was no such obvious answer to the question of why the kitten had been killed. Instead of finding a meaning I had to provide it. So I thought back over my day until I recalled a lesson I had learned earlier in the day about focussing my attention onto those things over which I had influence rather than worrying about matters beyond my control. I chose to dedicate the sacrifice to reinforcing this lesson, so that the resulting improvement in my life would be the tribute which would give value to the kitten's death. The precise mental processes by which I carried out this ritual are beyond the scope of this essay, but can be suggested by my closing oration to the dead kitten which was something along these lines.

"Kitten, I never knew you but I feel our fates have been bonded by my act of killing you. I regret this act, but seek in the solemnisation of it to transcend such regret. I therefore accept full responsibility for your death, and I dedicate its memory to reminding myself ever to focus my resolve towards those matters where I can exert influence rather than to dissipate my life in worrying about circumstances over which I have no influence or solution. Thus I intend that your death will for ever be a stimulus towards improving mine own life, and that my life will thus be ever a living tribute to your death and so to your life. Thank you, kitten.

One concern remains, however, which is that my decision was unilateral — you could not partake of it and might have chosen otherwise. But that is precisely an example of the problem I seek to resolve — I have no influence over your wishes as you are dead and gone, therefore I will not concern myself with them and will rather focus strictly upon my own intentions and reactions. I feel a lightening of my heart and I recognise that as a loosening of the bond between us. Go forth, kitten-spirit, you are now free."

The wording might sound a touch majestic for an off-the-cuff oration, but it is surprising how far the act of taking responsibility for death adds solemnity to one's utterances.

I hate putting this sort of thing into the book, because I know how it can be misread to confirm some people's worst fears about Magic. It does however illustrate the key feature, namely that one's own feelings and observation are the ultimate authority in Magic. It also underlines the importance of finding or creating 'meaning'. Although the sacrifice might appear ludicrous in Scientific terms, and blasphemous in Religious terms, what matters to me is that I appear to have made my peace and have not been haunted by the memory of those dead creatures which I offered as sacrifices — whereas I have indeed been haunted by other creatures that I have wronged.

The same principle extends to less dramatic examples. I am not a vegetarian and I try to accept some conscious responsibility for creatures and vegetables killed to feed me. The death is consecrated by my intention to cook well rather than create junk food. For some people the justification for the sacrifice is that "this creature died that I might live" — personally I find that disgusting because it simply trades my life for many others. I prefer to acknowledge that I could always skip a meal and so I am eating not to live but for pleasure. To me life is cheap — in a day or two any dead creature or even a piece of shit will soon be swarming with life — whereas joy is precious. Therefore I endeavour whenever possible to cook like an Artist, leave my plate clean and generally conduct my life as the sort of elevated being that I might myself choose to be eaten by.

CHAPTER FIVE
Fantasy worlds

It was described earlier how discussion between Magic and Science flounders because the idea of causality — so important in Science — has no bearing upon Magic. Similarly we find that the Scientific idea of existence is of no interest to the Magician. When the latter talks of a demon as being a "defect in his own pysche", the Scientist is likely to remark "so you don't actually believe that demons exist as such"; a remark which is quite meaningless in Magical terms.

Just as Magic theory avoids tangled arguments about causality by allowing causal connections to be total, so does it avoid existence arguments by assuming that everything exists.

Although this immediately saves the Magician from perplexing discussions as to whether the flying pink elephants that haunt him are real or not — and if not, why it needs a real psychiatrist to banish them — it is also a potentially dangerous step. For a universe in which everything exists is a much larger and more confusing one. In it, a muddled thinker might try to open a door with the memory of a key, buy Freedom in a shop, settle an argument with a dagger, or feed his cats on Love. In fact it is very necessary to have some sort of map or guide in such a universe.

The way in which Magicians map their universe varies from sect to sect. This fragmentation is probably partly the result of centuries of persecution, but also due to the very nature of Magic, so it would be too much to attempt a comprehensive description in this essay. Instead one example will be presented, an example based on the Cabalistic scheme of 'four worlds'.

The obvious beginning point to a Scientist would be the material world, as of that he feels sure. Thus it is that we have inherited from past Magicians attempts to describe the other worlds in terms of 'rarified forms of matter' — not always very satisfactorily, matter in itself being so rarified.

Philosophically matter is not such a good starting point. Eyewitness accounts of an event can diverge to the point that we can no longer trust 'seeing is believing'. A reasonable idea of the distinction between a phantasm and a solid object is that only the latter will withstand a long hard stare without decomposing. But in fact the distinction is only one of degree: experience suggests the brain maintains a visual image by making many small eye-movements. If you force yourself to stare fixedly and without blinking at an object, the image soon wavers and even vanishes until the eye breaks your restraint and moves slightly in order to restore the picture.

Even though there are circumstances when we cannot be sure what is material and what is illusion, yet at least we can be sure of our own experience of it at the moment of experience. Indeed for most of us, 'I think therefore I am' is a satisfactory starting point. So let us start with the world of everything that can be thought, everything that can be described, invented, imagined and conceived; a world of all our impressions, memories and abstract thoughts which we can describe or express. Let us call it the Mental World.

Within this huge and ever-shifting world, we soon distinguish certain types of thought which are slower and clumsier than others. These are the 'images'. Whereas the thought 'I wonder if it is time for lunch' can pass in a flash — hardly even verbalised, the corresponding mental images take a little longer: there is the feeling of hunger, the rapid memory scan of time elapsed since last looking at the clock, and the visual image of the clock itself.

These images form their own Image World within the Mental World. Examples of thoughts which exist in the Mental World, but without necessarily touching the Image World, occur in mathematics, eg the square root of minus one or the fifth dimension.

But within the World of Images, we find that some images are even slower and clumsier than the others; in fact they possess inertia. Although the thought of lunch was virtually instantaneous, the reflection on it took a second or two, yet the physical action of getting up and looking at the clock takes even longer, for here we are operating with the most solid and cumbersome impressions — those which form what is called the Material World. Experiences which take place in the Image World, but not in the Material, are called dreams or visions.

When considered in atomic terms, this Material World is itself extremely rarified, and so it is natural to ask whether there is within it an even solider world. What could be more solid than matter? The elementary particles themselves? In practice, we find that our experience of these particles is more of the nature of the Image or Mental World. It is as though the attempt to go down to something even more solid than matter results in a reflection back up to the less solid regions. Therefore we stop at this point and assume the Material World to be the last.

But what about the other direction? Is there a larger and even more rarified world which contains the Mental World?

From a logical point of view, it is convenient to assume that there is a larger world, simply so that any impression which does not fit the worlds described can be assigned to it. In practice it is this outer world which is most likely to be contested by Scientists; because if the Mental World comprises all thoughts which can be expressed or verbalised, then presumably the larger world would contain concepts which could never be expressed in words. Therefore we choose to irritate the Scientist by calling this higher world the Spiritual World, and we justify its existence by declaring that since it seems impossible to hold conclusive arguments upon topics such as Liberty and Love, then perhaps the words are simply labels for concepts which defy accurate verbal description.

The Spiritual World was called a 'higher' world. This is a further source of irritation to the Scientist who assumes that the word 'higher' is used as an indicator of value, ie as a Religious mind might use it. In fact it is only 'higher' in the sense of being larger and inclusive. A topologist would call it a 'super' space, but that sounds even more like a value judgement.

It is difficult for people of this age, who are used to considering thoughts to be a by-product of activity within the small box of our human skull, to see how those thoughts can form a world bigger than the material universe around that human skull. Here the idea of a shiny metal sphere, which contains as a reflected image within it the entire universe without, can be helpful. But a better analogy is to consider the whole of English literature and to see in what sense it is true to say that all such literature is contained within the twenty six letters of the alphabet, and still leaves room for all literature yet to be written.

(Actually, the above-mentioned difficulty could be lessening since the first edition of this book — see the essay Turds Made Fresh which discusses data compression and the unfolding of fractal universes from simple computer programs. It is published in What I Did In My Holidays.)

But a common reaction is to argue that the statement is simply not true, on the grounds of the Scientific belief that the material universe is an extensive reservoir of undiscovered facts which are slowly being revealed to us by Science. Such an arguer will say: "Your Image World doesn't contain an image of the far side of the Moon, does it? So that is something in the Material World which is outside the Image World." But of course the Image World does contain images of the far side of the Moon — an uncountable number of images of this as of any other unvisited place. Only knowledge can prune those images to find the one which corresponds to the so-called physical reality.

More subtly it can be asked whether the mind can be said to contain a true representation of the actual physical distance between here and the Pole Star. This seems tricky until you question what is meant by an 'actual physical distance', and find that the questioner is in fact confusing his own Mental World with the Material. If it were possible to travel over that distance, and so to experience it in that way, then the image of that experience would represent the distance. The distance can be expressed in the Mental World in so many words, or as a number of light years. To argue that this is not suffi-cient representation is to argue not about the Material World, but about a concept in the Mental World. In fact physical actions are the only arguments possible within the Material World.

On a higher level, it is likely to be argued that there exist images which cannot be described in words. For example, someone would ask: "Who has ever found words to describe the Mona Lisa?" However a television picture of the Mona Lisa, for example, is a description in words, the whole picture being transmitted in the form of a coded signal and then reconstructed. By an extension of this method, the image of the picture could be reproduced as faithfully as desired. Those who argue that the 'image' is not the whole picture are missing the point. It is the image which could be described in words: any indescribable impressions which accompany the image must belong to the Spiritual World, and so by definition, lie outside the Mental World of words.

So every object in a lower world is in one to at least one correspondence with an object in a higher world. For the chair you sit on
— so loved by homely philosophers — there is your corresponding
visual and tactile experience of it in the Image World. There are the
words 'the chair you sit on' in the Mental World, and there is a
concept in the Spiritual World which is touched upon when we ask
if the chair you sit on would be the same chair if it was re-covered or
put in another room.

On the other hand, every world contains objects which are not
found in any lower world. For example the Image World contains an
image of a tree with clocks growing upon it, swelling from little
watches to full size alarm clocks. This image corresponds to no reality in the Material World. Note however that, once pictured, it would
be possible to produce a partially satisfactory representation of that
tree in the Material World. It might look quite good, but would never
be the real living thing.

Moving up to the Mental World, I can produce the phrase 'time-
plated sky tomatoes', a perfectly acceptable choice of words and yet it
has no picture in the Image World. Again some vague visual representations float into view, of pale blue tomatoes in the sky, but they
fail to be really 'time-plated'.

In the Spiritual World, there is an ideal of which I am aware but
cannot describe. It can however be represented by the word 'justice'
in the Mental World, and by a statuesque blindfold woman with
scales in the Image World.

So now we have divided the huge and confusing world of all experience into four worlds, nested one within the other; the innermost
one being composed of matter. If anything lies outside those four
worlds, then it cannot be experienced — we need only call it 'the
Unmanifest'. In this scheme, matter is seen as condensed idea,
thought or energy, rather than images and thoughts being rarified
matter. With such a scheme in mind, we are less likely to confuse the
levels of reality, though different labels still allow for confusion in
discussion between Magicians.

Basically this is the scheme of the Cabalists, who see the universe
in terms of creation; 1) an idea touches us, 2) it can be expressed, 3)
an image or plan is formed, and 4) physical action results. But the
labels I have used are my own, or rather Johnstone's, for the purposes

66

of this essay. In other circumstances, I would call the Mental World the 'Intellectual World' because it is the world of mathematical concepts as well as of words. The World of Images I would call the 'Astral World' — a term familiar amongst occultists. However I realise that some people would disagree, calling my 'Image World' the 'Etheric' and choosing an 'Astral' world closer to my 'Mental'.

The disagreement is due to the possibility of choosing different boundaries. For example, we could simplify to only two worlds, calling them 'Matter' and 'Spirit', but that is too simple to be useful to the Magician. On the other hand, we could subdivide further, eg by a second fourfold division which splits the Material World into solids, liquids, gases and energy, and the Image World into: a) the most substantial delusions which actually deceive you; b) vivid dreams; c) normal mental images; and d) the most rarified images, such as an instantaneous view of all sides of an object, which cannot be held. And so on with the other worlds.

Alternatively we can disagree about the position of the boundary lines, preferring perhaps to exclude energy from, the world of matter, and ascribing it to an etheric 'force' world which includes our physical sensations and bodily urges.

In this way there have grown up many different divisions of reality, some into four worlds (or 'planes'), some into seven and some into more. Though sectarians can disagree upon terminology or definition, the basic idea or purpose of these classifications is simply that which I have described.

Thus it is useless to ask a Magician if God, angels or demons 'really exist'. Simply by saying the words, you have made them exist. Ask again whether these abstract entities can produce any effect on the physical world and they already have — they have caused you to ask questions.

While mentioning the different systems, it might be an idea to divert slightly and to discuss the use of the word 'dimension' in this context. Where I might use the phrase 'higher world' or even 'super space', some would use the phrase 'higher dimension', and this strikes me as unfortunate because 'dimension' has a definite and different meaning to most people.

The use of the word dimension is in origin like the use of the words 'ether', 'vibrations' and 'unconscious'. It stems from the

Magicians who feel the need to attempt to justify themselves with Scientific terminology. As will be explained later, a Magical theory can be built around any Scientific one; the trouble is that the Scientific theory moves on and leaves a Magical theory which is expressed in outdated and therefore ridiculous, Scientific language. First it was 'magnetism', then the 'ether', then the 'fourth dimension' and now the 'collective unconscious'. I must stress that each theory is perfectly acceptable as a Magical theory, but its language does not read well to an unsympathetic Scientist or educated person.

The idea of a fourth dimension suggests a model of the described higher worlds in terms of an increasing number of dimensions, hence. the use of the word by some Magicians.

Certainly the Image World contains four dimensions, for it contains time. Any past image can be considered alongside the present or future possibilities. What is more, there are some people who claim to experience fleeting fourth dimensional visual images, ie to see an imaginary object from all sides at once.

But the addition of one more dimension is insufficient to explain completely the extra size of the Image World: even within three dimensions it is bigger than the Material World. For the Material World is not continuous in space — the gaps between particles have no reality in material terms. On the other hand we can imagine the gaps between atoms, and any point in that gap, for the Image World is continuous unlike the Material World.

To a mathematician, the geometry of five, ten or an infinity of dimensions presents no more theoretical difficulty than that of four. As all his ideas are contained in the Mental World, we thus realise that the Mental World must itself contain an infinite number of dimensions. This is in accord with the theory of the 'Semantic Differential' where one would not expect to achieve total distinction after any finite number of steps.

As for the Spiritual World, well the very idea of dimension seems meaningless in a world where polar opposites appear to converge.

So for the benefit of those who prefer the ordinary use of the word, I have sketchily discussed my classification in terms of dimensionality but add the reminder that it is often used in a very different way, with a meaning more like my use of the word 'world'.

Having given an outline of the way in which a Magician might view what Scientists would consider to be 'fantasy worlds', it is necessary to suggest how he operates in those worlds.

Firstly he simply includes them in his field of observation. Here is another basic surprise for the Scientist who is likely to object to the word 'observation' being applied to a fantasy world. "What you mean is daydreaming!"

But surely observation cannot be complete unless it records all impressions which reach us? In practice we fall short of total observation; we have to be selective. The Magician is supposed to attempt to make note of any impressions which could be relevant to his working: although he may well stop short of his aim, it is likely that he will be observing much more than the Scientist who limits his field of observation strictly to the Material World. There are times when a Scientist would do well to admit certain subjective factors, especially when they reveal a strong desire for a particular outcome to his work.

Secondly the Magician admits that a problem in one world can often be solved in a higher world. Let us say that the problem is one of fitting a door in a confined space, and choosing a piece of wood for the job. It could be a lengthy business in the Material World, lugging all your bits of wood into position one by one to see if any one is big enough. It would be better to reduce the labour by working also in the Image World: just by picturing the shapes of some of your pieces of wood — eg discs and beams — you can see which ones are not worth trying in the gap. Even more certain is to work in the Mental World: measure your gap — ie reduce the problem to numbers — then go out and measure your bits of wood. If even that fails to find a suitable door for you, there might be a solution in the Spiritual World. Why a door? Why not a curtain? Do you really need anything?

Here the difference between Magician and Scientist is the extent to which this process is held to work. A Magician is more likely to assume, from his experience of the rapid growth in the higher worlds, that any problem must have a solution somewhere up the scale.

But probably it is of greatest interest to the reader to know what a Magician does when he works purely on a fantasy level — but here I add the reminder that it is not Magic unless in the long term there is a definite aim to such work — in particular what is meant by skrying or 'Astral Travelling'.

It is not easy to describe Astral Travelling without making it sound very glamorous. The reader who comes across accounts of astral visions should continually remind himself that the 'astral world' in such cases is the Image World that I have described.

Firstly the Magician needs a plan of his world. The scheme of the four worlds was called a 'plan', but really it is more like a side eleva-tion, showing the whole universe of experience divided into four storeys — don't let this slightly defective image obscure the fact that each of my worlds includes all the worlds beneath it — and what the Magician needs is a plan of each storey.

At first you might think of a map, and consider a globe of the Earth to be a good plan of the Material World. But where do nuts and bolts lie on that plan? Or hospitals? Or iron? Or stinking helle-bore? No, the sort of plan that is needed is one of those flexible systems of symbols mentioned earlier, a system like the Tree of Life of the Cabalists, or the tarot or astrology.

Again I will choose astrology as an example; although as a plan it is not so popular with Magicians at the present time, at least it is the most widely known of the systems, We will take for our plan the planets of the astrologers.

The first objection is how can you call it a 'plan', for it is only a list of planets? The answer is that, when studied, the planets of astrology (and the elements of any Magic symbol system) exist not just as isolated boxes, but stand in definite relationships with one another: Venus and Mars are in a polar relationship which parallels Moon and Saturn or Jupiter and Mercury. So in a way which is unlikely to be clarified within the scope of this essay, the choice of the seven plan-ets does in fact provide a plan of our world. This plan will be applied to the Astral, ie Image, World.

Day by day, working in all worlds, the Magician constructs and reinforces the association with his chosen plan in the way which was suggested in an earlier chapter. Should he feel a bit ignorant, or lack-ing, in any one planet, he will study the relevant correspondences. Let us say that he is least sure about Jupiter or cannot see what is its essence. Then he should attend a few wine parties, study jovial people and experience their company, or else attend some open air sports functions and ask "If you subtract the Martian elements, what remains?"

The state to work towards is that in which every item in your Image World, and therefore also the Material, is immediately ascribable to the relevant planet, and inversely that the name of the planet is able to evoke a whole subworld of relevant images. But even before that state is reached, the Magician can attempt astral working. The process is one of controlled day-dreaming, the control consisting largely of the original choice of what region is to be explored.

The Magician arranges circumstances conducive to day-dreaming, ie a quiet, secluded and comfortable place. He also arranges the place so that it will set him on the right lines: if his chosen region was that of Venus — or a more specific region such as 'Venus in Libra' — it would help to choose a rose garden or a boudoir. Failing that, he would merely decorate his room with a few Venusian items. Very often the Magician merely makes sure that there are no violently antagonistic circumstances or effects around him, and then proceeds to direct his day-dream simply by using appropriate mental imagery. He might visualise a pink silk curtain before him with the symbol for Venus embroidered in pastel green, and commence his daydream by stepping through the curtain to a world beyond.

For many people, the first experience of the astral plane is disconcerting, not for its vividness but rather for its feebleness. Unless they are gifted with exceptional powers of imagery, they do not find themselves swept into a vivid and dramatic dream-world.

Close your eyes and you do not immediately banish your surroundings. You still have a feeling of the room around you, and its position in your world. How strong is that feeling? Can you actually visualise each item of furniture and mentally walk around the room? Now try to imagine that you are really in a different, but equally familiar, room, Can you again clearly visualise the new room in all its detail? Or can you merely produce a vague 'feeling' of the other room with a few fleeting visual images of parts of it?

For many people the first astral experiences are no more vivid than that feeble feeling. The Venus world has to be willfully constructed around them, and constantly rebuilt as it fades. What is more, they never lose the feeling of the original room in which they are sitting in the Material World, even while the day-dream progresses. Their thought stream runs more on these lines: "There's the curtain. Now what ought I to find on the other side? A rose garden on a warm sunny day, I think. Okay, here we go . . . yes, here's the garden around me. I should be able to smell roses I suppose . . . yes, that's better. What else ought there to be? The sound of bees and singing birds? Yes . . . damn, I forgot to leave a message for the milk-man . . back to the rose garden . . I suppose I could do it tomorrow morning . . . where are the birds? It's about time I met an occupant of this world — a young girl in soft silk clothes . . . " And so on, each part of the scenery being put in its place because it ought to be there.

But without necessarily growing more vivid, the dream does with practice come to life. It begins to exhibit spontaneous elements which on later consideration are in keeping with the Venus symbolism, and can be checked with the experience of other Magicians. Should any doubtful entities be met in any sphere, then there exist traditional tests which can be applied and which will either banish the entity or else confirm its validity. The Magician can also meet a guide in his travels who will show him around the world and answer questions about it.

Thus the Venus world which started as a sort of mental filing cabinet in which he placed appropriate symbols, has become a new coherent world of experience, and one in which the Magician can learn. What he learns about the world of Venus will, when meditated upon after the journey, teach him lessons about the corresponding elements in everyday life.

If it seems hard to believe that such a collection of symbols can 'come to life', it is as well to consider what often happens when people become interested in psychology. If Freud is their teacher, they begin to have Freudian-style dreams. At first, these are likely to be imitative, a construction of other people's dreams which have been described in books, but soon they will experience their own Freudian dreams, ie the world of Freudian symbols has 'come to life'.

One way to improve the initial vividness of these 'daydreams' is to share them. The 'pathworking' is a magical group exercise where, typically, everyone closes their eyes and visualises while one member of the group describes the inner journey. The results are usually far more vivid and coherent when done in a group — and when you go home and try to repeat the exercise on your own it can be a bit disappointing.

In this brief essay, it would be unwise to go too deeply into Magical terminology, simply because these terms are subject to a wide variety of usages. But I would like to mention the terms 'angel' and 'spirit', 'archangel' and 'god' as used in modern Cabalistic Magic.

Entities which exist primarily as Images are called 'spirits'. Some such images are specific to certain areas of the Image World, so we find in our exploration Moon spirits, earth spirits (gnomes) and so on. Such traditionally well defined regions of the Image World tend to develop (or develop from?) a prime spirit called the 'Angel' of that region. There is also a negative counterpart called the 'Demon'.

Similarly in the Mental World, there is a president of the equivalent region called the, 'Archangel', and in the Spiritual World, there is a 'God' of that region.

So when we set out to explore, say, the Image World of Air, we would tend to invoke or pray to the God of Air as protector — this is analogous to getting permission from the highest authority. Yet we would only expect to meet the Angel of Air in our journey.

In fact any appearance in Image of an entity claiming to be an Archangel or God should be regarded with deep suspicion. Even if it is 'true' as a 'message', it should be realised that the Image is only a 'representation' and therefore imperfect. The more proper appearance of an Archangel is not a clearly defined image, but a shifting and hazy one — more like an attempted image of my 'time-plated sky tomatoes' or the 'square root of minus one'. The appearance of a God is more marked by a sensation of great awe, or numinosity, rather than any describable image.

These terms are given as examples only: although these are common meanings, some writers may use the words in a different sense. The book Words Made Flesh contains an interesting analogy between this angelic hierarchy and the hierarchy of programs which might be needed to create a virtual reality. It considers a virtual field of grass — each individual grass plant in the virtual reality has its own software representation (its 'spirit'); all those plant spirits are derivatives of a program which identifies that particular grass species (the 'angel' of that species) and it in turn is a derivative of a program which defines grasses (the 'archangel' of grasses) and that is in turn a derivative of a program which defines vegetation (the 'god' of vegetation).

When considerable experience is gained of all the worlds (to omit knowledge of any world would be to lay yourself open to the danger of unrecognised elements from that world invading the others), then the astral equivalent of Ritual Magic can be attempted: a ritual is enacted or action taken, in a higher world which is intended to precipitate a desired event in the Material World. The mechanics of this method are of no interest to the practical Magician, though so intriguing to the Scientist that he will soon perceive or project them himself. When the Magician asks his Venusian guide to "make Amanda marry me", and the Venusian guide says "I will if you obey my instructions: first you must wash yourself all over and put on clean fresh garments..." then the mechanics will seem laughably obvious to the Scientist.

This account of astral working is likely to offend people of two extremes. First it will offend those whose imagery is so vivid and powerful, and whose astral travels are so successful, that they will object to the idea that the astral world is 'only a day-dream'. To such people I reply that I disagree with their use of the word 'only'. It is the fault of Scientific education that they think that a day-dream is necessarily trivial; remember that in the account here given the Material World is 'only' that small part of the daydream world which is capable of standing up to certain tests.

Secondly it will offend those whose imagery is so feeble, or nonexistent, that they will not believe such day-dreams to be possible.

Someone with a name like Galton around the turn of this century investigated the differences in people's power of imagery and found there was a full range, from those who did not even believe it possible through those who had fleeting black and white images which could not be held or scrutinised, to those who could visualise so vividly that they were actually able to open their eyes and 'project' the images in order to see them as if through their eyes. Although his work was inconclusive, it did suggest a possibility which seems intuitively quite likely: that the more abstract thinkers such as mathematicians were less likely to have good visual imagery, or conversely that clear visual imagery is likely to obstruct abstract thought or reason.

In this context, it is interesting that the original pictorial Chinese characters were at one time expressly formalised and obscured in order to make them more suitable for abstract use, Furthermore, this idea is in keeping with the idea that a surfeit of toys is likely to obstruct a child's imagination, or that too much intellect is a bar to spirituality. In each case, an excess in one world is a hindrance to experience in the world beyond it.

There is a Magical theory which states that a 'male' is positive in the Material and Mental Worlds, and negative in the Image and Spiritual Worlds (and vice versa with a female), and thus it is that our 'male' scientific thinking is likely to neglect imagination and spirituality in favour of material and intellect. A balance of the 'male' and 'female' is symbolised by the caduceus of Hermes with its two snakes crossing the central staff as they pass upwards through the four levels.

So do not think that there has been any exaggeration when I say that it is possible to train yourself to have instructive dreams, or even for some people to have them spontaneously (cf C G Jung's "Memories, Dreams and Reflections"). On the other hand, neither must you think that it in any way belittles the astral world when I describe it in terms of day-dreams. Is there any idea or invention in this world which was not foreshadowed in a daydream?

In this chapter it has been explained that, although it is literally true to say that the Magician works in the realm of fantasy, it is misleading to say so unless there is also an idea of how those fantasy worlds relate to other people's ideas of reality.

CHAPTER 5A
Whose fantasy?

The cover notes of the first edition of SSOTBME read as follows:

Lemuel Johnstone was often accused of being an original thinker, yet he himself maintained that his ideas were utterly in keeping with the traditions of a less dogmatic past. Now the reader can judge for himself, as this essay presents a concise and elementary account of his theories on the nature of Magic, and is an excellent introduction to the subject for the intelligent layman. It will also be of interest to those who have some knowledge of Magic, because no-one was better able than Johnstone to describe traditional Magical doctrine in the context of modern life. In this account Magic comes closer to all of us, without losing its fascination.

It is a rare pleasure to find a Magical writer who does not limit himself to an indulgent 'ripping away of the surrounding veils of mystery and illusion', but who is prepared also carefully to restore those veils lest there be any doubt that the subject is indeed Magic.

What message was being conveyed by this? Why, for a start, the use of the past tense? Why restore those 'veils of illusion'?

The writer was clearly concerned about a tendency which has become even more extreme since the book was written: the tendency for a book to become more important than its content or its author.

There always has been some imbalance. I recall an elderly Irish poet neighbour telling me of his dream which was to be sitting opposite a stunningly beautiful girl in a railway carriage and to discover that the book which is absorbing all of her attention turns out to be a volume of one's own poems. I too was brought up in the tradition that an idea for a book was a compensatory gift with which a less than gorgeous human being might reduce members of the opposite sex into melting adoration — ie that an idea, and a book should be tools to serve the writer.

What Johnstone noted was a tendency for the idea and the author to become subservient to the book. The correct approach to a publisher nowadays is not to send a manuscript or book proposal, but rather a good-looking photo of oneself plus a professionally produced curriculum vita outlining one's claim to fame. Then, maybe, mention an idea for a book. This is because the author is now seen as a tool to sell a book — something to be hyped and paraded in public so that any sort of volume with the name on it will be sold. In both imbalances, it is the idea which takes last place.

In this case the author was exploring the difference between the way we read books by dead or living authors. When the author is dead, do we read more respectfully, knowing that nothing more can come from this pen? When the author is living, do we become distracted by the living presence, wanting to put down the book and question or challenge the author for ourselves? Johnstone wanted to step back from his ideas, retreat into anonymity and allow them to be studied in their own right without the irritation of an author and the reader's fantasies surrounding him.

Being considered as 'an original thinker' is a vital part of being groomed as a vehicle for selling books — and yet it was something that Johnstone eschewed. He was more keen to present traditional ideas in a fresh light than to replace them with something new. And yet his ideas often do seem new.

For example, at the beginning of the 1970s he was suggesting that the basis for our reality might be neither matter, nor energy but simply information — ie that we could be living in a 'virtual reality' to use a term which did not appear until many years later. This is an idea which is still considered revolutionary.

But Johnstone did not see it so much as a new idea but rather as a handy modern metaphor for an ancient tradition that our reality is an illusion or 'maya'. Note how, in the previous explanation of the four levels of reality, the worlds of archetype or idea are seen to come before solid matter. At each stage — from spirit to concept, from concept to image, from image to matter — there is a change of state which is comparable to the difference between an underlying software and the experience of virtual reality it can generate.

Plato had his own metaphor to describe this virtual reality: it was of a cave upon whose inner wall shadows are cast from the light shining into the cave. In this model what we call 'the real' world is those shadows cast by the reality behind us. What Johnstone considered was simply the television tube as the modern version of the cave — we live out the soap opera world cast upon the phosphor screen and are barely mindful of the stream of data directing the movements of the electrons hitting and illuminating that screen. In the case of a computer screen, that stream of data is itself a product of the software which lies behind it.

In my additions to this text, notably in the following chapters 6A and 7A — I expand upon the idea of a virtual universe because it does indeed provide a very useful metaphor for Magical theories. But what is not intended is that the reader should be ultimately seduced by the metaphor. In Words Made Flesh I propose a walking meditation in which you imagine that the world we live in is a virtual reality programmed into a great computer and you go about life looking at it as a bit of clever programming — noting how cleverly and how smoothly colours, textures, perspective, tastes and other phenomenon have been built into the experience and how realistic are the other characters in this world. In this way you begin to experience the Magical continuity and coherence of existence. Then you remove the original prop and abandon the idea of a great computer — stop imagining it but try to hold onto the Magic it invoked.

This process of 'pulling oneself up by your own bootstraps' is not allowed in Scientific thinking where a model based upon a false premise must be invalid — but it is no problem in Magical work. So what is here being suggested is that we accept the cybermagic arguments as a technique for overcoming the resistance to Magic which current materialistic models of reality impose upon us — but that we should not fall into a new form of restraint by insisting that our world 'really is' a computer simulation.

All you need for Magic is a belief that world of the senses is not 'all there is' and that there is some underlying level of reality — archetypal forms, thoughts, information processing, natural laws or whatever — which can be manipulated to alter or shift this illusion of experience.

CHAPTER SIX
Miracles

To unsympathetic ears, the answers given by Magicians seem evasive. In this booklet I find myself more often trying to explain why it is useless to ask certain questions than actually answering those questions.

"Can you perform miracles?" is a harmless question, for we never cease from performing them, but "can you demonstrate miracles?" is the most boring question known to Magicians.

Go up to the veteran car owner who has spent ten years resurrecting his beloved De Dion Bouton from a pile of rusting scrap, and ask him how much it's worth or how fast it goes, and you have no more chance of triggering a warm reply than if you ask a Magician to demonstrate a 'miracle'. In both cases, experience has taught that the question itself probably betrays the asker as one who will never see the point. So often it is the sign of either the opening of hostilities, or else of the hungry thrill-seeker who begs always to be surprised and delights only in announcing that he is not.

As before, the question will not be answered but dismissed at length. For secretly, strictly between ourselves, Magicians too find the reasons for its dismissal somewhat intriguing. Many a tickle-ribbed hour can be passed listening to Scientists who — whilst repeatedly acknowledging Occam's Razor as their guide — yet prefer to suggest a complex barrier of trickery, mechanical gadgetry, obscure human motive and of course illusion, rather than admit the one alternative possibility... that they do not know everything.

In view of our education and our strong resistance to the miraculous, is it not itself a miracle that people still believe in the supernatural?

How can we fail to believe in miracles when there are so many recorded in history? Once there was a simple answer — that they were all lies; now it is suggested that self-deception, imperfect memory and wrong conditioning are to blame.

So does that mean that only dimwitted people ever 'see' miracles? Alas, no. Even otherwise intelligent and well-educated people like Jung and Crookes occasionally succumb. We are none of us perfect.

But the fact that 'well educated' people of our century see fewer miracles than do primitive people is seen as confirmation that they are in fact aberrations of the mind.

To the Magician this is rather amusing: the fact that in order not to see miracles we have to be taught not to see them. It is also a little sad for us moderns who have had such teaching thrust upon us.

The Scientist who prefers not to accuse people of lying believes that primitive people see magic only because they are taught to believe in it, yet in many cases he overlooks the possibility that we might *not see* magic only because we were taught *not to believe in* it.

Once you have gained an understanding of your own defenses, it is interesting to study them in others, for they exist on more than one level, Easiest to observe is the intellectual resistance to the miraculous.

Critics of mystery delight in pointing out that the human mind likes to remember selectively interesting coincidences — a fact which seems hardly remarkable, and yet overlook the more surprising fact that we often ignore these coincidences.

Keep a diary and note your dreams. Select a few examples which seem to illustrate the popular idea that dreams are based upon a reordering of the past day's experience. Very often the connections are fairly tenuous. Take half a dozen such examples, and you will be able to convince most people that dreams are a re-hash of the day's impressions. Now reverse your examples in time and present them as a case for precognition — you will be laughed out of court.

Lemuel Johnstone once attempted to quantify people's relative resistance to the miraculous by increasing the number of examples in the second case until they were considered as 'proof' of precognition in the same way as they had previously been 'proof' of memory. In whatever way he shuffled his examples he found a curious fact, that the more he presented the more ludicrous his case seemed.

A similar effect was observed on a television programme about flying saucers over Oxfordshire, England. An expert was asked to comment, and his criticism relied heavily on what might be called 'the craze factor' — ie he pointed out that no saucers were reported

80

until the sighting got into the news, and then there was a flood of reports. This to him was evidence that the whole thing was a mass hallucination, and he apparently did not think it necessary to consider other possibilities. Surely if there really were flying saucers, just the same thing would happen? Once one report hit the news, people who normally stayed indoors would go out and look at the sky. Again note the double standard: whereas in Science repeated observation is seen as confirmation of Truth, in any other field it is seen as confirmation of hallucination.

So what happens when we see a miracle? The answer is that we see a 'conjuring trick'. But what if trickery is ruled out? Of course it never can be, but even then we can call it 'an hallucination'. After Uri Geller had bent his spoons, many people were relieved to hear conjurors announce that they too could do it. So relieved were they that they never bothered to subject those conjurors to any stringent tests. As Houdini showed, the best publicity any conjuror can get is to claim that he can duplicate others' achievements. Perhaps the discovery that a conjuror could fool them would be too embarrassing?

Instead of being skeptical about the conjuror's claims, Scientific investigators actually rely upon the conjurors to help them to arrange impossible tests for the supernatural. The attraction of the conjuror to the Scientist is that he is the embodiment of the Scientific belief in human gullibility and deception. Science asks the paragons of deception to lead it to the truth. (See a later essay The Charlatan And The Magus — reprinted in Blast Your Way To Megabuck$ With My SECRET Sex-Power Formula — for a more profound exploration of the role of trickery and deception in Magic, Science and life.)

We are protected from the miraculous by the comforting possibility of rational explanation. To suggest that there could ever be a miracle story capable of breaking through that defence is to suggest that there is a finite limit to man's power to invent. So there comes a time when we grow bored of trying to outrun reason, and instead wonder what happens when we are actually witness to a miracle situation. This is more difficult especially since it is now less easy to find people who do not believe in hypnotism.

The technique used is called 'post-hypnotic suggestion'. It is possible to hypnotise a person, and tell him that he will obey certain commands or perform some action spontaneously, after he has come round from the hypnotic trance. In this way it is possible to confront someone with a miracle and watch his reaction.

A favourite example is to say that a certain person in the room will vanish when one command is given, but will reappear when another is given. So it is possible to present the subject with a human who will vanish and reappear instantly before him. But, to your disappointment, the subject does not shriek: "My God, Joe's vanished", he merely looks away. If you ask him where Joe is he will not tell you "he vanished before my very eyes", but will make some very ordinary reply like "Joe went out" or "Joe must have gone". When Joe instantly reappears, he will merely say "ah, you're back". For his mind will cover up the miracle by superimposing a normal exit and return. As far as his conscious mind is concerned, he has not witnessed any miracle but simply Joe's comings and goings.

The next experiment is to force him to stare directly at the invisible Joe and therefore to see what is behind him. You will find that the subject will think of many good reasons not to co-operate, but if you force him to, say, read a notice while the invisible Joe stands before it then you will be sorry to find that you yourself are unable to see miracles. For the subject will appear perplexed and the suggestion will break down. You have been saved.

No matter how bizarre you make the subject's action under posthypnotic suggestion, you will find that his mind can devise a rational explanation. A shy young man will stand up in the middle of a lecture and shout 'hot stew!' without any justification. But if you ask him why, he will be unlikely to say that 'dark forces compelled him'. If he is rational, he will believe that he did it to prove to himself that he was not in an hypnotic trance, or some such reason.

Why is it so important for us not to see miracles? In discussion of such subjects, you will find that some people not only do not believe, but are actually 'disturbed' that anyone could still believe in the miraculous. Once you have made a devil, he has the power to frighten you. But this fear also exists at a more basic level.

A colleague once was privileged to find someone who really did not believe in hypnotism, and still did not believe after many demonstrations. A whole room full of people vanished and reappeared around the subject repeatedly, without his turning a hair. Then my friend remembered a similar case which had been described by a medical hypnotist, and so he caused half of a person to disappear. The result was not "oh well, you've convinced me now", but something closer to a nervous breakdown.

The rational view of the world is ultimately a logical one. To admit one little miracle or inconsistency into a logical system is not as harmless as you might think. It causes complete disruption.

An example of such a logical system is arithmetic. If we obey all the rules of arithmetic but allow just one wrong result, then any wrong result can be proved. Let us say that we allow that $5 + 7 = 10$, therefore $12 = 10$, therefore $12 - 10 = 0$, therefore $2 = 0$. Divide both sides by 2; then $1 = 0$. This means that all numbers are now equal to 0 (eg multiply both sides by 100 to get $100 = 0$), and therefore all equal to each other. In other words the whole of arithmetic collapses if we admit one single illogical result into the system.

So when something in a rational mind takes such pains to avoid a confrontation with the miraculous, it is not being awkward or deceptive, it is defending the consciousness from total chaos.

Try not to see this personal adjustment of reality as a fraud, for the concept of fraud is merely a projection from Science's 'shadow world'. At every moment, we are surrounded by a multitude of impressions, so it is necessary to be selective if we are to cease meditating and start taking action. A city dweller is not continuously aware of the sound of traffic, or the starlings, and yet he will catch the faint tinkle of a coin dropped on the pavement. It is necessary to be selective.

If a racialist is convinced that all Negroes are unintelligent and bestial oafs, and yet he watches a discussion programme involving well-educated Negroes, it will merely confirm his opinion "who the hell do they think they are putting on airs like that". If you take a Scientist to a spiritualist seance, the better the show the more it will convince him that the whole thing is a fraud.

Somewhere in our mind, a censor sifts the impressions in order to guarantee a comfortable and consistent mental environment. It is not a swindler: it is more like a loving aquarist who provides a goldfish with water, plants and artificial rocks to make it feel at home. That is why some people call it 'the Guardian Angel'. Until you come face to face with this Guardian Angel, your world will not change.

In order therefore to pass from being a Scientist (and so rational) to being able to see miracles, it is necessary to pass through an intermediate state. There is a name for the intermediate state; it is called 'insanity'.

But unless you have passed through that state, what proof have you that it is only intermediate? Looking towards Magic, Science sees only a fog which it calls 'insanity', and as is often the way with Scientific terminology, the word itself is mistaken for an explanation. We assume that once Science has a word for it, then we know all about it.

So don't ask a Magician to demonstrate miracles. You will never see them until you cease to be what you are, ie you will never see them.

But what of those people who have witnessed miracles? What happened to their defenses?

A miracle is only a total disaster to a rational thinker. If by nature you are a 'feeler' rather than a 'thinker', you can happily survive a few inconsistencies. However you are unlikely nowadays to suffer very large inconsistencies because whatever your natural bent you are likely to have been educated as a thinker — and I mean more than just education gained in the classroom. Therefore your Guardian Angel might allow you a few bizarre events, but will probably save you from witnessing anything which is likely to make you into a social misfit. As was explained earlier, the modern Magician can hope for runs of luck or some 'amazing coincidences', but he should not expect too many gold coins to materialise from thin air. Especially not if he is by nature talkative.

In this context it is interesting to wonder whether it is the strength of Scientific beliefs which gives them their power to unify our experience: is Science the safest way of all? (See the later essay Magic In The Eighties — reprinted in Blast Your Way To Megabuck$ With My SECRET Sex-Power Formula — for a discussion of the notion that an ability to bend metal is not a 'higher power' so much as an atavistic failure to maintain metal as solid as we need it to be.)

The Artist has no need of beliefs, he only adopts them if his thinking moves into the philosophical Religious sector, and he creates a new Art movement. In the Religious sector, belief is seen as a virtue;

we strive to believe. By the time we come to the Scientific sector, effort is no more for belief has become automatic: no-one is more rigid than the rational materialist. Yet Scientific progress suggests that beliefs must be changeable. This is the attitude of the Magical sector; beliefs are altered to suit circumstances. A ritual Magician chooses his beliefs in the way a Scientist might choose his apparatus, At the extreme we have systems like that of Austin Spare where all belief is condemned as limitation and bondage. Free from all belief we are back to Art. Anything can happen to an Artist.

So, can Magic defy physics? The world waits with bated breath for my answer — and I proceed to evade the question. But here is a miracle; some readers will think that I have answered the question.

Naturally everything that I have written has a perfectly reasonable alternative explanation . . .

CHAPTER 6A
So, can Magic defy physics?

I gather that, three decades on, the final paragraph of the last chapter needs elucidation. At the risk of spoiling a good joke, I'll have a go.

The relevant point of misunderstanding between Magic and physics is that physics assumes a physical reality and Magic only assumes an illusion of physical reality.

That does not mean that Magic undervalues the physical world as some Religions appear to. The word "illusion" does not have negative connotations in Magic because all is considered to be an illusion. So saying "matter is maya", or "an illusion created by Hermes the Trickster" or whatever is really just an invitation for matter to "join the club". Quite a compliment, really.

There have been many attempts to portray this illusion of reality over the millennia, but I'll stick to Johnstone's model of a virtual reality as it is even easier to grasp as the century ends than it was when he first proposed it in 1970.

THE MODEL

For a fuller explanation see Chapter 7A: but the basic idea is that universes will tend to evolve within an 'information soup' as internally structured information systems in a manner analogous to the way intelligent life-forms are assumed to have evolved from a 'chemical soup'. Just as with the evolution of complex life-forms, it is the complexity of the internal structure that offers certain survival advantages. Thus an information structure which models an inner universe with consistent physical laws and its own evolved life forms will compete better for the processing power of the information soup.

Now the problem arises when we move from the outer appreciation of this virtual reality to an inner experience of it.

Take the Mandlebrot set program in my Mac computer as an example. This 'contains' a two-dimensional world of infinite size and uncountably infinite complexity of detail. Because it represents a universe defined by continuous equations, it is infinitely bigger than the small program which contains it; but it is only unfolded from those equations screen by screen as an outside intelligence calls them up. Although infinitely rich in content, it has only two dimensions and no time dimension — so it cannot include its own models of intelligent life as our universe does, and it depends upon outside intelligence to unfold it.

Our universe does have a time dimension, and it can and has evolved to contain its own inner information processing systems. Some of these brains have evolved — as did the universe itself — sufficient complexity to model their own inner universes. This could be a disaster for our 'macrocosmic' universe as it could lead to 'looping' of the program as the inner 'microcosms' modelled the macrocosm itself. The macrocosm has survived, however, by evolving a defence against such cancerous eruptions, which is to isolate sufficiently complex microcosms by imparting an illusion of 'separateness'. Each microcosm is tolerated because it now feels itself to be separate from the macrocosm.

This sense of separateness is what we experience as 'consciousness'. This point of self realisation by a universe has been symbolised in various ways over the ages as twoness or multiples of two. For example:

1) George Spencer Brown in The Laws Of Form describes an elemental 'split' from which a complex system evolves — oh bugger, I cannot find the book on my shelves to quote. That means I must have lent it to someone so many years ago that I've forgotten and have no chance of recovering it.

2) The I Ching describes how all manifestation arises from an initial division of the Tao into two principles Yin and Yang and thus into the multiples eight and sixty four and so on.

3) Those who see the universe as a devilish illusion symbolise this by giving the Lord of Duality two horns.

4) IHVH in the cabalistic system is a fourfold formula for conscious manifestation translated as "I am that I am"

And so on. (I am still angry about that missing book. It can be a close friend for years and yet you only have to look away for a decade and it is gone without a trace. Life is a bitch.)

Thus we have described three levels of experience. Firstly, to the macrocosm it is the processing of digital information. Secondly, what is being modelled is a smooth universe based on continuous mathematical equations. This smooth reality is only experienced by conscious microcosms, and they, thirdly, experience it only as binary digital information. This is like the way I only experience the continuous Mandlebrot set in my computer when I invoke it as pixellated screen images — only in our reality the consciousness lies within the universe that it perceives. So also the physicist who wishes to pin down which slit the photon passed through can only do so by destroying the wavelike continuity of light. (I should explain that this model evades Penrose's argument in 'Shadows of Mind' because it places consciousness not within any algorithmic program but in the relationship between the micro cosmic program and the macrocosm which contains it).

Magic, then, is to 'surf' the unconscious continuity of existence until a desired state is sensed and only then is conscious attention allowed to seize the outcome. Whereas Science uses conscious attention to stay within the digitised, particulate perception of the universe, Magic only uses that sword when it wishes to break the continuum.

THE EXAMPLE

You are in a taxi on your way back from a late night party. As you turn into your road you note the taxi meter reading just over four pounds so you reach in your pocket for cash and find it EMPTY!

Horror! Nothing to pay the taxi with. You face a crisis and you take Magical action. For example:

1) You might have a belief that the universe is basically benign and will look after you. So you outwardly or inwardly cry "help! I haven't got enough cash!"

2) You might have time to perform a traditional Magical act such as Spare's sigillisation technique, clutching a talisman or whatever.

3) You might assume a benevolent deity — say Mammon, Jesus, Jupiter or Ganesha — and offer devotion to it in return for help.

Whatever your Magic, you now sit back with a hopeful sigh and your hand brushes against something hard in the crack at the back of the seat. There are five pound coins nestling there! You now have the money to pay the driver.

Now a really bold Magician can just accept that the Magic has worked, that the surfing stopped just at the point where coins would be found in the seat. There is, however, a strong tradition among Magicians that an operation should end with a banishment.

A typical inner banishing ritual goes as follows. "That's a bit of a coincidence — that I should find just the right coins to pay the fare just as I needed them. On the other hand, I cannot believe I would have been stupid enough to set out in a taxi without checking I had cash — even after a party. I bet those coins were in my pocket all along and simply fell out as I sat in the taxi because of the rake of the seat. Yes. That must be what really happened."

Banishing Magic in this way is actually quite good Magic. It is only dangerous if you come to 'believe in' this explanation, or start to congratulate yourself for 'seeing it'. Just as it would be equally dangerous to boast to others that you can make coins appear at will. In Western Magical tradition we are encouraged to cultivate four 'powers', namely to know, to will, to dare... and to keep silent.

CHAPTER SEVEN
The nature of Magical theory

The question of the miraculous was only considered very sketchily partly because it is not very important to a practicing Magician, but also because it is unwise to appear to be trying to convert people to Magic. As was explained, a single coherent world-view is a precious asset, bestowing all the benefits of what we call 'sanity'. The purpose of dealing with the subject at all is identical to the purpose of this whole essay: it is to present a modicum of encouragement to those for whom the Magical way of thinking would be natural, and for whom the pressure to conform to apparently (to them) ludicrous Scientific fashions is unpleasant. Such people need few words about Magical effects. A more important topic is Magical theory.

Unless the nature of Magical theory is understood, it is very easy to get the impression that Magical theory (and for that matter Religious theory) is forever being defeated by the progress of Science. In view of the conclusion reached in Chapter Three about the independence of the four systems of thought, it would indeed be strange if Science was able to defeat Magic in this way (or vice versa for that matter). But the mistaken belief that Science is at war with Magic or Religion apparently leads many people to despise Scientific progress as though it were an act of aggression. Thus we find people, often associated with fey Religious or spiritualist sects, who betray anger in the face of Scientific theory in such words as 'what nonsense to reduce Love to a chemical reaction in the body'. Very often they simultaneously reveal that they have a lot of the qualities of a Scientific mind: their apparent rejection of the theory scarcely conceals a total belief in it, or resignation to it, and goes along with a belief that the whole world is going downhill (in Chapter 3A this is explained in terms of a legacy of skepticism in Magic).

The idea that an equation of Love and a chemical reaction means that Love has somehow been reduced to a chemical reaction seems to be peculiarly characteristic of the modern Scientific mind. It is peculiar because it is not obvious how it should arise via a process of logic and observation; possibly it is a hangover from Religious thought of previous ages. Or is it another symptom of the mistaken belief that Science can wage war on other ways of thought?

To the Magician Love is incapable of being reduced. I deliberately write the word with a capital because I am assuming its full significance as a representation of something in the Spiritual World, so how can it be reduced? The Alchemists, for example, were forever equating Love to chemical reactions, but they never kidded themselves that they had reduced Love in the process. On the contrary, the equation could be better said to elevate chemical reactions, revealing in them a representation of that indescribable Spiritual idea. Aleister Crowley was just one example of a Magician who would be relieved when the turgid psychoanalytical theories of Love give way to a chemical revival.

What then makes us wrongly believe in the defeat of Magical theory? It is a lack of understanding of the nature of such theory.

Magical and Religious theory is 'perfect', that of Art and Science is 'imperfect'. Scientific and Religious theory is 'progressive' whereas the Artistic and Magical is not.

The imperfection of Scientific and Artistic theory means that it is forever changing: Science, being progressive, makes advances whilst Art theory goes round in cycles. The perfection of Magical and Religious theory makes them immune from that sort of change, yet only Magic is completely static. Religion has a sense of progress akin to that of Science but more like a ripening process than the revolution of Science.

The progressive parameter is open to argument: some would say that Religious theory makes no more progress than does Magic. But provided I am careful to distinguish between the actual theories, and the spirituality of their followers, I still feel that I can detect progress in Religious ideas — for example the evolution towards monotheism. Others will point out that Science has cycles of fashion as much as does Art: you cannot debate with a nutritionist without first asking whether it is protein, carbohydrate or vitamins that are 'in' this season. But here again I would prefer to distinguish between, as it were, Science and science. When a system degenerates (eg through lack of competition), there is a tendency for it to become tainted with elements of its polar opposite system (or 'shadow'). Thus a philosophy adopts talismanic symbols and becomes a 'religion', and then as it degenerates it develops characteristics of Magic: a Magician has the danger of being obsessed by his beliefs, which are meant to be temporary expedients, and they become a 'religion' or 'god' to him. Similarly Art can degenerate into a process of observing what the public wants and following the logical conclusion (ie a Scientific method); and Science (particularly in the hands of the marketing professional) can degenerate into 'High Art', either pursued for its own sake or else used to decorate our conversation and justify our whims.

However the 'progress' issue is less relevant here. What matters is that the theories of Magic and Religion are 'perfect', that is to say they belong to what was called the 'Spiritual World', and so are beyond language. This means that true Magical theories are very simple, very abstract and universal in their scope.

It also means that they are practically useless, for how can you apply a theory which cannot even be put into words? The answer is that you must find a verbal representation (as was described in Chapter Five) which can be applied. It is the mistake of assuming that such representations are the whole theory which leads us into wrong ideas about Magic.

Magicians themselves compound the error when they 'fall' in the way described above, and start to worship their chosen beliefs: if you meet someone who insists that flying saucers really come from the objective out-there planet Venus, then you cannot call him a Magical thinker. Indeed such people often share all the narrowness of vision of the Scientist despite a few gaps in the logical linkage and would better be called pseudo-Scientists. His theory is vulnerable to attack by Science, but only insofar as it falls short of being a Magical theory.

For any theory which is capable of definite Scientific disproof is not an example of Magical theory. A survey of Venus could determine whether material flying saucers came from there; this is not a Magical theory. However 'flying saucers are messengers from a higher intelligence' could almost form part of a Magical theory because there are no clauses about objectivity: the 'higher intelligence' could be within one's own brain, or it could be a sociological or universal gestalt. But it is not a very good example of Magic theory because it is too limited in scope, merely devised to emphasise a comparison.

A better example is the theory of the four elements Earth, Air, Fire and Water: a theory which survives untouched by the irrelevant discovery of over one hundred chemical elements, a theory which has physical, sociological, psychological, in fact universal implications. I cannot explain exactly what the theory means; I can only draw attention to other representations. It can be seen as an observation about four states of matter (solid, liquid, gas and plasma), as a plan of psychological types (as in the system of Jung) or as a key to the divisions of the Zodiac. Myself I have experienced it in forms more subtle than any of those representations. For in place of 'proof of' a Magical theory, we have 'experience of' it. And in place of 'knowledge of' it, we have a 'feeling for' it. It would be unremarkable to find that an un-westernised Polynesian had been aware of the idea of the four elements all his life without ever having heard of the theory, whereas it would be sensational to find that he had sophisticated opinions about general relativity without ever having heard of Einstein's work.

The four elements theory is a truly Magical one, being very simple (stemming from a division of all phenomena into four categories which stand in a certain relation to each other), quite universal and utterly perfect. If asked to explain it further, I would either succumb to a natural twentieth century love of verbiage, or else have the wisdom to present Magical theory in a Magical way — saying "go away and observe Earth, Air, Fire and Water for a year".

Aleister Crowley gives a number of such Magical theories in Magick In Theory And Practice — he calls them formulae, as in 'the formula of tetragrammaton'.

So Magical theory lies beyond the reach of Scientific theory, but does this mean that it also lies beyond the reach of those of us who feel surrounded by Scientific theory?

The chapter started with a reference to the frustrated Magician who feels uncomfortable in a Scientific world: if such a person has had the usual Scientific upbringing, he will perhaps bless me for my good intentions, but ask "is it not too late, now that Science has so altered the world that there is no longer any room for Magic or Religion?"

To such people I can confidently assert that, provided the Magical way of thought is natural to you, then the seeds of Magical theory can take root in whatever world Science is capable of putting around you. Less charmingly, the finite processes of Scientific method are not

SEVEN - THE NATURE OF MAGICAL THEORY

capable of forming a network fine enough to exclude all possible representations of a Magical theory. To such theorists all Science can do is to erode certain over-precise representations of a Magical theory: a sad process it is true, but it does help one to transcend inadequate models.

Possibly the best way to explain how this works in practice is to give an example in a little more detail, but in so doing I must ask more hostile readers to be patient. As should be clear by now, it is impossible to discuss a Magical theory without first 'freezing' it to a single, less adequate, interpretation, and it is of course even more impossible to condense the full reasoning behind any one example into such a short essay.

One day Johnstone was describing to his friends the Magical theory of the Universal Mind: usually expressed in terms of Microcosm and Macrocosm, there is a common Magical idea that mind, or consciousness in some form, extends throughout the universe.

Johnstone explained how this idea had survived despite changing beliefs. When electrical forces were felt to be the explanation of all phenomenon, the Universal Mind was seen as an all-pervading tide of 'etheric forces'. At another time it was seen as an effect of vibration, a sort of 'music of the spheres'. When the 'fourth dimension' captured our attention, then the obvious place for the Universal Mind was in another dimension. Thus it is that Magicians have always felt free to say that a flower turns towards the Sun because it 'wants to'.

But one of the audience took exception to this last point saying that it was ridiculous now to say that a flower can 'want' when it has no brain or nervous system: it faces the Sun because the sunny side of the stalk grows more slowly and so curls the flower in that direction, a mechanical process free from notions of desire. All Johnstone's examples were set in past ages when the Scientific vision was still incomplete, Only now did we know enough to have totally excluded the concept of 'purpose' from natural phenomena.

The process had been a gradual one: when Newton initiated gravitational theory, he eliminated the belief that objects 'want' to fall together. So Physics and then Chemistry were the first to be purged of the idea of 'purpose' or 'desire', everywhere replaced by a simple mechanistic principle. Next was Biology, when the idea of an 'aim' or higher purpose was eliminated from the theory of evolution, and now at last in Psychology the Behaviourists have shown that we do not even need the idea of 'will' or 'purpose' when considering man himself.

Now it is known that even thought has a mechanistic explanation. Thought is the working of a very complex computer, ie the brain, so any human mind and the sum total of its dreams, experiences and impressions could be duplicated as long as the structure of its pattern of cells was accurately modelled in a sufficiently complicated computer. Even those thought processes which we still believe to be uniquely human will become noticeable, or reproducible, as our computers grow more intricate. For along the line of progression between the simplest computer and the most ingenious and creative brain, there is no qualitative gulf, only a gradation of complexity.

Therefore 'purpose', 'will' and 'desire' are meaningless fossil concepts, as are the 'spirit', 'inspiration' or 'creativity'. How then could Johnstone still believe in Magic, and in particular in his 'Universal Mind'?

First Johnstone pointed out that it would be unreasonable to expect him to answer on the spot, because that would force him to reproduce in a moment what could only in practice be an evolution of belief. So it was after tea before he replied.

As soon as he began to talk about 'purpose', he was interrupted and asked what precisely he meant by the word. He retorted, some-what irritated, that he did not see how his friend could claim to have eliminated purpose if he did not know what it meant in the first place, that any normal human knew the meaning of the word from his own experience, and that all his friend had demonstrated was the unfortunate necessity for the human brain to first reduce itself to mechanical idiocy as preparation for the Scientific method.

The rest of Johnstone's argument should by now be obvious: the Scientist sees no purpose in mechanism, and so according to present theory deduces no purpose in his brain; the Magician detects purpose in his own thinking, and so according to the same theory deduces purpose in mechanism.

If we are happy to note phenomena called 'purpose' and 'desire' in our own brains, and we are reliably informed that the progression from the simplest computer to our brain is simply a progression of increasing complexity, with no qualitative gulf, then surely it is equally true to deduce that the rudiments of our own thought exist in the simplest computer as it was to deduce that our own thought can contain nothing which transcends the working of such a computer?

So once the Magician has satisfied himself by observation that purpose exists in his mind, and the Scientist has informed him that his mind is only quantitatively superior to that of an IBM computer, then surely he cannot deny the elements of purpose to the IBM without placing a qualitative gap somewhere along the line of evolution between it and our brains?

So the fact that I can distinguish purpose in my own thinking means that I can grant the rudiments of that quality to thoughts of any computer once I have accepted the claim that my mind is a phenomenon which would be duplicated by any electrical, fluidic or mechanical linkage which matched the pattern of the network of cells in my brain structure.

But surely everything in Nature is a computer? Any network, from a tangle of wires to a flow of traffic along intercommunicating roads, can be seen as a logic machine or simple computer. Even a single free particle in space is a computer because: a) any change in its motion illustrates a computation of the resultant of the forces acting upon it; and b) according to another of Newton's laws, its continued motion serves as a 'memory' of the resultant of the previous forces which have acted upon it.

It is pardonable therefore to see the quality of mind everywhere in nature, especially as a larger computer is formed when any two or more simpler computers interact with one another (a field of grass, a turbulent waterfall or a wood, is a very complex computer, indeed, too complex to be fully modelled by even our most sophisticated computers to date). If 'mind' is the unavoidable by-product of such interacting systems, then all of Nature is a mind, all of mankind forms a mind, the whole universe is a mind. If mind is no more than a pattern of information interaction, then mind has existed long before the creation of this world.

Reincarnation demands no more than the possibility of the pattern which forms my personality being approximated to in later brains, or other larger patterns. Although the large number of elements in any such pattern might make the possibility of its duplication seem statistically infinitesimal, the likelihood is greatly increased when one realises firstly that any one brain is complex enough to 'contain' an arbitrarily large number of personalities (this is most obviously seen in some cases of madness, but also in the case of a novelist who lives his characters), and secondly that personality is not an exact quantity (for I am a very different person in the early morning than I was the night before, but I consider both to be me.) Thus it is that Austin Spare could unearth experience of animal incarnation, by exploring his unconscious, for does not our brain share its ancestry with theirs? To the Magician consciousness is much more of an absolute than the objective reality of the Scientist. So when by suitable mental exercise and years of practice he finds that he can 'remember' when the pattern of his own mind was for a few brief aeons being reproduced in the swirlings of interstellar dust, he has little time for the Scientist's question "but you can't prove that you really were Napoleon, can you?"

It is only necessary to outline the idea as above; once the way of thinking is indicated the arguments are obvious. And yet it is all just a game — showing how the Universal Mind reappears in a computer theory. It is no better than calling the Universal Mind a 'higher vibration': in fact experience may show that the latter term will remain the more useful to Magicians.

Do I really believe in this computer theory? The question is a symptom of Scientific education: 'really' and 'believe' are not words which go happily together in Magical thought. I suppose that there are many Scientists who 'really believe' in a computer theory of the mind simply because it is possible to witness their projection of that belief. As Johnstone noted, such theorists often adopt an intellectual approach of "I don't know what you mean by 'purpose', 'art' or 'inspiration' and therefore I cannot talk about them." In other words they do reduce themselves to something less than a human (for few humans have qualms about such words). Similarly we note how the 'computer world', ie the academics, technicians and businessmen concerned with computers, does appear to adopt the characteristics of a computer world: their published papers show the influence of computer language being notable for their large number of nouns — often of a formal type with standard endings like '-ation' and '-ology', and very limited choice of verbs. Thus it is meaningful to ask such people whether the theory is 'really true' or if they 'really believe' in it because we can see how they are in the process of making it true. The adaptability of the human mind is such that we can just as gracefully imitate the workings of a computer nowadays, as we were able to behave like fallen gods in the past.

But to a Magician it is a complete waste of time to wonder if the theory is really true, Probably even before this book finds a publisher, someone will have devised a new theory of consciousness and this argument will already be out of date. But who cares?

And if some people see the example as mere verbal trickery, pointing out that it "has failed to prove that there exists an external, objective force of 'purpose' which guides Nature", then they should look back to the devil theory of Chapter Four. Whoever first asked whether purpose could be external and objective? It was not the Magicians.

Why is it necessary to emphasise that the Magician should not worry about trying to prove his theories are true by other people's standards?

It is easy to laugh at a crank Magician who has become obsessed by one of his theories, without understanding how strong have been the temptations leading up to that obsession.

The Magician starts by considering representations of some theory in the light of his own experience until he forms an idea of, or feel for, the theory behind the representations. Then he decides upon his own version of the theory, which may or may not be an original interpretation, and studies how it applies to some practical purpose.

Lemuel Johnstone had a feel for the theory of the four elements. He also had a desire to explain his attitude towards Magic to unsympathetic friends. Accordingly he devised his theory of four ways of thought, based of course on the four elements. But he only used it for that purpose as he took steps to save himself from obsession.

Unless you have some form of defence — whether it is cynicism or magic circles — there is a tendency for your idea to begin to accumulate evidence. (Presumably this is because 'evidence' is what we believe in today; in the past the temptation might instead have been a 'sense of righteousness'.) You find that more and more facts begin to fit, and what started as a mere working tool is beginning to look like the Key to the Universe. Of course there is also the temptation of personal pride at this point, especially when you start to collect disciples — for the beginnings of obsession bestow great personal magnetism. In his autobiography, Jung describes such a process of temptation when coincidences seemed to add up to a suggestion that he had a Great Message for Mankind. In his case, it was a Scientific background that saved him: he could not believe such a thing possible, so he survived and his life's work was the better for it.

In the case of the Magician, the ultimate defence is to remember that any version of a theory which lies within your comprehension, and in particular one that can be expressed in words, is necessarily not the whole truth. So however well it fits the facts — indeed especially if it fits too many facts — it is necessary to grow out of the theory once it is no longer needed. This is exactly analogous to the 'license to depart' in Ritual Magic: when a spirit has been evoked for some purpose, then it is necessary to disperse it again. Failure to do so would be likely to result in obsession.

This is why Magical writing often piles on the self contradictory paradoxes, for example the chapter called "Onion Peelings" in Aleister Crowley's "Book of Lies". It also explains why the Magicians that hit the headlines can give such a poor impression of Magical doctrine, for it is the falling stars that make the most amusing press stories.

Finally I should add an example to illustrate what may well be obvious by now: that the very qualities which make a Magic theory invulnerable to Scientific attack also make sure that the theory is of no use in Scientific work, indeed it is usually meaningless in Scientific eyes.

It has been a bad day: your shoe lace broke on the way to the office, you missed the bus and were late. So you sit at your desk and sigh: "Oh dear, what next? Things always happen in threes."

'Things always happen in threes' is a representation of a Magical theory, a weak one it is true because very incomplete. At first glance it might seem a very definite and objective statement, one that could be considered or even tested Scientifically. But no, how can Science distinguish the third happening?

As you sit at your desk, a multitude of things are happening; cells are dying in your brain, molecules are bombarding you, cosmic rays piercing you. Outside the window you see the rain pouring down.

You see a girl with a strange look in her eyes put down a shopping bag and fumble in it. She looks up and down the street, then walks briskly away. Your conscience tells you that you ought to rush out and catch her to tell her she's forgotten her bag. Damn: that means that you'll have to get wet again. So you must act without any delay so that you don't have to run too far. But as you get up, the phone rings. Hell: some bad news perhaps?

As you hesitate between the phone and the door, there is a flash and a blast that hurls you across the room.

The third thing has happened — a terrorist bomb. You know it, and so would anyone else who heard your story. But not if the story was considered in a Scientific context, for in those terms there have been millions of happenings, and it is far from clear why the mind should choose to claim that there were only three.

What might have appeared to be a precise and logically verifiable statement is in fact inextricably bound up with the subjective ideas of importance of events.

The conclusion to be drawn from this chapter is that it is often a mistake to bring one's full powers of analysis to bear upon the words of a Magical theorist. Very likely his use of words has an individual bias, and so it is necessary to make an effort to see what simple principle lies behind his utterance. Once the principle is sensed, it should be tested in one's own experience before being accepted. Then it may be necessary to form from it your own imperfect version which may resemble that of the aforementioned Magician, or may appear quite different.

All this may seem terribly hard work compared with the direct acceptance of Scientific theory at face value, but it should be remembered that in Science it is likely that the hard work has already been done, for it is necessary to have the appropriate training in order to fully understand a Scientific theory in the first place. (Actually, I think I have improved upon this in the present edition because I explained in Chapter 3A that the value of a Magical theory lies not in its falsifiability but in the ability of the Magician to believe it.)

Once one has become accustomed to the nature of Magical theory, it will be found that the theories are quite independent of your varying beliefs about the structure of the physical world. They are like an all-pervasive virus.

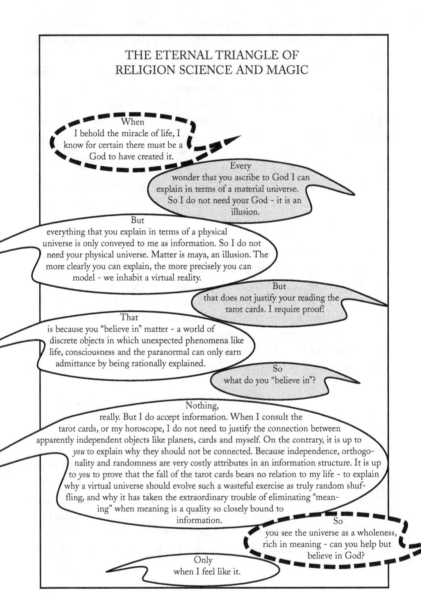

THE ETERNAL TRIANGLE OF
RELIGION SCIENCE AND MAGIC

When
I behold the miracle of life, I
know for certain there must be a
God to have created it.

Every
wonder that you ascribe to God I can
explain in terms of a material universe.
So I do not need your God - it is an
illusion.

But
everything that you explain in terms of a physical
universe is only conveyed to me as information. So I do not
need your physical universe. Matter is maya, an illusion. The
more clearly you can explain, the more precisely you can
model - we inhabit a virtual reality.

But
that does not justify your reading the
tarot cards. I require proof!

That
is because you "believe in" matter - a world of
discrete objects in which unexpected phenomena like
life, consciousness and the paranormal can only earn
admittance by being rationally explained.

So
what do you "believe in"?

Nothing,
really. But I do accept information. When I consult the
tarot cards, or my horoscope, I do not need to justify the connection between
apparently independent objects like planets, cards and myself. On the contrary, it is up to
you to explain why they should not be connected. Because independence, orthogo-
nality and randomness are very costly attributes in an information structure. It is up
to *you* to prove that the fall of the tarot cards bears no relation to my life - to explain
why a virtual universe should evolve such a wasteful exercise as truly random shuf-
fling, and why it has taken the extraordinary trouble of eliminating "meaning" when meaning is a quality so closely bound to
information.

So
you see the universe as a wholeness,
rich in meaning - can you help but
believe in God?

Only
when I feel like it.

CHAPTER 7A
Cyber-animism, the virtual universe and pseudo-scientific jargon

In Chapter Six it states that the cybernetic arguments of Lemuel Johnstone 'should be obvious by now', and yet — nearly 30 years on — few people see them as obvious.

Johnstone took the concept of conscious intelligence as a property emerging from data processing complexity and deduced the likelihood of such intelligence emerging everywhere in Nature. Thus he sought to reinstate animism which is such a useful Magical theory. Unfortunately, however — as suggested in my later essays — our culture's long rejection of animism has made it hard for Western society to accept his idea of artificial intelligence in the first place. We find it hard to accept the idea that a computer could ever be self conscious and possess a 'soul', whereas in Far Eastern cultures — with their more recent animistic traditions — a computer could have a soul just as easily as a car, a rock or a stream could.

This gives rise to a circular argument, something that is anathema in Science but quite acceptable in Magic. Circular arguments are fine for Magic because Magic is more concerned with changing perceptions than ultimate truth. A circular argument can be used like a grindstone, not to 'prove' but rather to erode resistance to an idea

Let us begin with someone who cannot accept Johnstone's cyber-animism because he is, for example, a New Ager who resists the idea of artificial intelligence. I then apply the above argument "if a quartz crystal, a tree or a spring might contain a deva, might not there be one resident in a very complex computer?" Nothing has been proved, it has just become slightly 'easier to accept'. I then suggest "if that dance of data within silicon could invoke an intelligence, might not similar dances of data throughout nature invoke a whole angelic hierarchy of devas analogous to the hierarchy of routines within an operating system?" I then suggest that "if our entire physical universe is thus permeated by such a field of consciousness, surely you cannot deny some element of that awareness to a computer created within it?" and so on. At no stage is artificial intelligence 'proved' but rather it is made to 'feel nicer'.

For a serious Magical act, however, there should be some benefit or purpose. I have long justified cyber-animism as a useful alternative to conspiracy theories, because it allows us to ascribe 'spirit' to systems. I recall a rationalist long ago attacking my thesis by saying "there is no such entity as 'Science', there are only scientists". Although I have *defined* Science (as well as Art, Magic and Religion) not as an entity but as an inclination in this essay, nevertheless I have felt free to talk about it in familiar terms as an entity which can evolve and compete like a living being in the ecology of human culture. That is to say I can address it as a spirit with rudimentary survival intelligence which is related to its human practitioners but also distinct from them. So, for example, when Science produces discoveries which threaten human existence, I need not assume that there must be an evil Scientist who wishes to destroy us, but I can rather explore the survival value of a way of thought which both poses threats and promises solutions.

Conspiracy theories are surely another example of decadent Scientific thinking: "for any phenomenon there must be a cause and, as Science denies the agency of spirit, then evil can only be a product of human malevolence". So when (in defiance of all that is known about placebos, human suggestibility under stress and the mind-body link) the medical profession encourages legislation to replace healthy outdoor images on cigarette packets with warnings of death — I do not assume an evil clique of doctors who are seeking to destroy our health, but rather I recognise the survival intelligence of the 'spirit' we call 'the medical profession' in generating new threats to health to keep pace with the cures with which it buys human attention and devotion.

A more recent example. Late twentieth century economic success has been uneven — the rich getting richer and the poor poorer. When I hear a 'fat cat' from a privatised utility justifying his bloated wealth with the sentence "but it's a free market", I feel angry and wish to take his kind on a Concorde trip across the Atlantic and, halfway across, announce "good news, everybody, we are now in a free aeroplane! I've just killed the pilot!". However, I can reduce this burden of anger more effectively by realising that it need not be individual greed but rather the nature of Money that is at fault. In our business culture it is those who have the most wealth (eg the board of directors) who decide how future money should be distributed. No matter how well-intentioned and fair minded the individuals concerned, this is a mechanism which is biassed towards the aggregation rather than the spread of fortunes. Money, as we have allowed it to evolve, has become a herd-animal and I do not happen to be at a place where it has herded (perhaps I should sacrifice a goat to it!).

Thus a Magical theory of pantheism, a world peopled with spirits, is really a practical version of a theory of systems which recognises autonomy in processes. It would have helped the libertarian movement in Thatcher's government to realise that you do not necessarily further the freedom of the individual by giving greater freedom to systems such as industry, commerce and finance.

This approach was justified for its usefulness. It has been useful to me in providing understanding and replacing suspicion and anger with more useful emotions and potential solutions to problems. I also wished to spread these benefits to a wider public in my writings, but have learnt a practical lesson instead. I have discovered that conspiracy theories can be better friends than Magical solutions because they attract better media coverage and so greater wealth. That is why I have decided to write no more on the subject.

VIRTUAL REALITY

Instead I say a little more now about the ancient and widespread Magical theory that matter is an illusion or, to put it in more modern terms, that our reality is 'virtual'.

As explained earlier, Magical beliefs are chosen to support a desired end result. If you want advice and you have a tarot pack, you adopt some form of belief that a tarot pack contains or else is a doorway to greater wisdom, and then you draw the cards.

So it is desirable to select beliefs which offer greater scope for Magical results. The belief that our world is but a shadow play of mighty cosmic forces, which can be wooed and manipulated by human wisdom — that is a pretty good Magical belief. The belief that the world was made by one God who forbids the use of Magic is a less useful one. One of the worst possible Magical beliefs is that our world is made of solid matter shaped only by chance, within which human consciousness and will arise as mere epiphenomena. Magic-wise it's utter useless crap, and yet it is a belief heavily endorsed by our Scientific culture. So what is needed for modern Magic is a belief which will subvert Scientific materialism and restore the unreality of matter.

The candidate that Lemuel Johnstone put forward was the notion that we are living in a cybernetic virtual reality which has the laws of physics programmed (or learnt or evolved) into it. The strength of this magical belief is that it does not attempt to oppose the materialistic model so much as to transcend it. This was originally explained in the following terms.

1) If reality is ultimately materialistic and rational, then it could be described in a finite set of instructions and modelled as information.

2) If it could be modelled in this way, then it will be — at the very least because, given limitless time, all possible permutations of a finite universe should occur.

3) For every one original reality there will be many such sub-models, and they too will generate many sub-sub-models.

4) The nature of complex systems means that it is almost impossible for any reality to reproduce itself exactly, indeed there is greater likelihood that

the submodels will be mutations of the original, subject to different structures and laws.

5)Because the models severely outnumber the original reality, or realities, it is therefore more likely that we are living in a universe modelled as information, and it is most likely that it is not identical to the original reality.

6)Thus Johnstone's Paradox: *if reality is ultimately materialistic and rational, then it is highly unlikely we are living in a materialistic, rational universe.*

His ideas, like his universes, spawned their own variations. One, championed in Words Made Flesh, is that it does not matter whether reality is ultimately material, energetic or information-based, all that matters is what we believe it to be, and information will become the most likely candidate. Another version described in later essays, like my "Response to Shadows of Mind", is that the universe does not actually have magic programmed into it but, like any software, it has bugs which sometimes allow miraculous or paranormal phenomena. In this version the software of the universe is self-debugging and that consciousness has a key role in this process — if you witness a paranormal event, the more you seek to capitalise upon it by calling in witnesses or scientific researchers, the less likely it is to be repeatable, because such conscious attention is a trigger to the de-bugging mechanism. Note that, because Johnstone's model places consciousness not within the algorithms of artificial intelligence, but rather within the relationship between those algorithms and the containing universe of information, Penrose's Godel-based counter-argument has no relevance here.

The object of presenting this information model of reality is that it is a useful basis for Magical belief. The above mentioned books spell out how the argument can be used to justify any paranormal or magical principle you wish — from reincarnation to tea-cup fortune-telling — so I will give only one example here of the technique. Let us go for a biggy and 'prove that God exists'.

DOES GOD EXIST?

Let us assume an apprentice Magician who is attracted to Paganism and so wants to believe in a Great Spirit or Great Mother or whatever of the universe, but has difficulty because of his Scientific education. As far as he is concerned Science has 'disproved God', so how can he get over this hurdle?

1)We begin by testing the strength of Scientific disproof, to give us a measure of the required strength of the new belief.

What we discover is that Science has not delivered strict proof of God's non-existence, so much as to make him unnecessary. For every demonstration of the reality of God by a Religious person — eg how could such a complex and well-ordered world exist without a creator? — Science responds with an alternative non-deistic explanation — eg the theory of order emerging from random complexity.

So 'God is not necessary' does not need 'God is necessary' to counter it. 'God is more likely' will be sufficient.

2) Next we avoid the temptation to look for bigger, better weapons of counter-argument. Instead we simply borrow the same weapon and return fire. The psychological advantage (remember, we are working within the Magician's psyche) is this: the return fire either hits home or else, if it does not, then it casts doubt on the validity of the original argument.

Thus we argue that the material world is not necessary, using the same argument as above: any aspect of material reality which the Scientist can demonstrate to me can be reproduced as information. The Scientific explanation is only valid insofar as it is precise — and that is the precise quality needed to render it exactly into information. Therefore I do not need the existence of material reality, I believe only in virtual reality.

3) Now today's Magician quite likely accepts the idea that complex order can evolve out of chaos, so we cannot use the nineteenth century Religious 'watchmaker' argument at this stage — the one which says 'if this is a virtual reality then someone must have programmed it'. Instead we explore the modern notion and use it as a metaphor.

The most complex emergent manifestation in modern mythology is that, from a random chemical soup, there emerged self replicating forms which in turn evolved living cells which in turn evolved complex living structures which in turn evolved consciousness.

So we explore this analogy. We conceive instead a random information soup. In place of competition for chemicals or territory we conceive competition for processing power or memory, and see how recurring calculations such as infinite series could evolve in analogy to crystal structures, and how these would gain advantage in an information soup. We also conceive that programs with more flexible internal structures could also evolve and replicate (in analogy with viruses) and have even greater competitive advantage. And there would be further advantage in those programs which aggregate into complex information structures which model their own inner universes, because they would be self motivating like living organisms. So a virtual reality like our universe could be just one of many similar or diverse universes that have evolved within the information soup, and it owes its survival to having evolved a set of 'physical' laws and constants which is consistent with a stable and competitive universe — just as the internal structure of the higher animals can be shown to have evolved by enhancing their survival.

In the biochemical model, however, the most complex organisms have evolved consciousness, which presumably must have some survival advantage. It is not unlikely, therefore, that the most complex universes in our information soup will also be conscious, as it would give them similar survival advantage. So it is quite natural to assume that our universe is a conscious entity, and that its mind is what we call Great Spirit or whatever.

4)To summarise: the Disbeliever and the Magician can now be conceived as two blood cells within my body. The Disbeliever is claiming "I have flowed all over Ramsey Dukes from head to toe and have not witnessed a single cellular process which cannot be explained in terms of simple chemical or electrical reactions. I do not believe this body is conscious because I do not need it to be." Whereas the Magician states "I too have explored him from head to toe and do not see why such a complex structure would have evolved without having also evolved a measure of consciousness. I therefore find it easier to believe that Ramsey Dukes is conscious."

As suggested, it is no more a strict proof of God's existence than was the original a proof of non-existence. It has simply tipped the scales of likelihood to make it easier for the Magician to choose the desired belief which is, in this example, that Nature is a conscious spirit or god.

This suggested model of God is only appropriate to such nature-religions. Of course the argument would need to be refined for those Judeo-Christian sects which demand of deity a long beard and white robe.

PSEUDO-SCIENTIFIC JARGON

I'm in a bit of a dilemma as to whether to include some more words about the way that Magic can pilfer Scientific terminology to deliver functional Magical metaphors. On the one hand I feel it is an irritation which can usefully be salved, on the other hand I fear that I may be spoiling a lot of fun.

It is so delicious listening to Scientists fuming over New Age or theosophical pseudo-scientific jargon, that I really do not wish to deprive future Magicians of this pleasure. My own favourite phrase in face of pompous Scientific dogmatism about, say, lack of hard evidence for the benefits of vegetarianism is "but, of course, [*insert topic of discussion*] is known to vibrate at an altogether higher dimension". Discerning readers will appreciate the exquisite juxtaposition of that brutal 'of course' with the rapier-like incoherence of vibrating 'at' a dimension.

So it is only the comfort of realising that no Scientists will ever read my books which permits me to append a few explanatory words which I wrote under a pseudonym as a guest editorial for the 'Energy' issue of the magazine "Caduceus".

"I Just Love Your Energy, Baby, It's So Relaxing"
Reflections on meaning, vibration and essence
A friend of mine was answering an advertisement for a massage couch and wanted to know if it had a metal or wooden frame — as she "preferred the energy of wood".

Her phrasing suggested some sort of nuclear experiment where the atoms of first a wooden then a metal massage couch were smashed into energy while a team of observers watched from a distant bunker. After the second searing blast my friend turns to the tester and affirms that she definitely liked the first blast better.

I was amused by her use of the word "energy", but that doesn't mean I rejected it. I understood perfectly clearly (if not precisely) what she meant by her words — and communication is the main job of language. She had used the word "energy" in what I would describe as a magical rather than a scientific way.

The statement "this car has a turbocharged engine" conveys precise technical information. But when the word "turbo" is written in big letters across the back of a car it conveys a whole lot of additional information about style and image — the word has become, say, 40% scientific information and 60% magic. But when "Turbo" is written large on a bottle of aftershave, it becomes 100% magic. Some people would insist that the word had lost all meaning — but that is hard on the cosmetics company which probably spent thousands of pounds on that trademark.

A word does not need to have meaning in order to convey meaning. I can shout "fascist" at a power hungry politician even if he is a member of the Labour party. The poet Gerald Manley Hopkins can write of "betweenpie mountains" and "wimpling wings" and get away with it.

To me scientific language is the use of words for the meaning they have, while magical language is the use of words for the meaning they convey as metaphor.

Science is itself a good source of these magical metaphors. In the early nineteenth century magnetism caught the public imagination and a whole raft of magical theories of "animal magnetism" and "magnetic passes" were floated. Then science postulated an ether and spiritualists took up the idea of "vibrations" and "etheric" fields and forces. This century brought the idea of a fourth dimension, adding "dimension" to the magical vocabulary. Now we have a spate of literature which weaves magical theories on the basis of quantum terminology.

If you insist on the original scientific meaning of these words, the result can be highly amusing. To the cynic it looks as if science has moved on and left a bunch of cranks trying to justify themselves in terms of outmoded terminology: sensitives wittering about "etheric vibrations" at a time when the ether concept was no longer recognised by science; talk of "higher" dimensions without any explanation of how a dimension can be "high"; the phrase "negative energies" when energy is normally recognised as a scalar quantity.

But if you admit the metaphorical use of these words the result is much more informative.

Barbara Brennan's interview in this Caduceus is titled "the Four Dimensions, AIDS and Sound". It is clear that Barbara's dimensions are not those of Einstein when she describes the first dimension as "the physical".

Meanwhile in this issue we have Atum O'Kane describing four kinds of magnetism which I would defy the most sensitive of magnetometers to register. Notice too that he writes "...the dimension of energy or magnetism..."

This issue of Caduceus, like the last, focusses on the theme of "energy", yet it clearly covers subjects way beyond the remit of the Minister for Energy.

When my friend said she preferred the energy of wood, she meant that she felt better with it than with metal. This sounds more like an information than an energy exchange — a point made here by David Spangler in his article "Making the Energies Work For You". Dr Taylor referred, in Caduceus 21, to the idea of a "scalar field" which carries information but not force — this too sounds much more like the sort of "energy" described in these pages.

"What exactly is this energy?" is an interesting question. But remember, it may not actually be the crucial question.

CHAPTER EIGHT
Secrecy

When the system of patents was first devised, the idea was not that it should provide a means of keeping other people from using an inventor's ideas, but rather as the word 'patent' suggests, that it should encourage inventors to make the ideas accessible for the inspiration of others. This institution might well be seen as the turning point when technology banished the influence of Magic and became the playground. of Science. For secrecy is as useful to Magic as it is inconvenient to Science.

Secrecy in Magic is not just a ploy to irritate Scientists. It is an important part of method. But its importance is so much a matter of experience that it is almost impossible to explain the importance to those who lack that experience; it will therefore only be considered briefly.

In Chapter Three, reference was made to Science's body of accepted truth. As Science only works outward from that knowledge, it is naturally important that its full extent should be available to the Scientist. The total is too large ever to be needed by one researcher, but every part must be available in case it is needed. Not only does it slow down Science's progress if certain areas are secret and have to be separately reconstructed by other researchers, but also when wrong conclusions are drawn through suppression of the necessary experimental evidence, then the effect is positively harmful to Science.

This means that secrecy is so undesirable in Science that Scientists are liable to be extremely scathing about Magical systems where secrecy has its place.

Firstly it must be remembered that Magic does not require a body of accepted objective knowledge, and so the virtues of free expression, so obvious in Science, are considerably reduced in the case of Magic.

Secondly, however, it must be realised that secrecy can make a positive contribution to Magical method. Though sometimes forgotten by modern Magicians, an old axiom of the Hermeticists required that their initiates should 'know, will, dare and keep silent'.

Astrology is perhaps the branch of Magic closest to the Sciences. An astrological conference seems therefore to be very much like a

Scientific conference: it is an open affair with lectures and discussions on all astrological topics, with a free passage of knowledge. However, it has an additional feature not expected in a true Science, for not only are there different branches of Astrology, but there are also different schools. Here lies the difficulty, for all goes well in a lecture on a different school until actual contradictions of method are reached. Of course, apart from Magical explanations of this, there are also simple psychological explanations — after all, certain branches of Psychology suffer from the rivalry of different schools — and so there is no hard feeling. However, there will always be found some astrologers who come away from such an affair reeling under the impact of several schools, and despairing of the total complexity.

Whereas two separate branches of Science tend either to be mutually irrelevant, or else to add up to something even greater, there is a tendency for two Magical systems to be mutually destructive. This is not always as dramatic as it sounds: in the case of the astrologers it simply means that when a member of one school comes into contact with another he might find that he is temporarily a confused and less positive astrologer.

It was explained in Chapter Seven how the practical application of a Magical system requires a temporary effort of belief in it. Practical Scientific work requires a narrowing of the observation to essentials and an opening up to the full theoretical possibilities. Practical Magic work requires a narrowing of the theoretical possibilities but a wide open receptivity to observations. This is the point where rival systems can be harmful.

In this essay I described matter in terms of a condensation of spirit or thought. If one was planning a Magical operation based on that idea, it would only be confusing if one came across an interesting speaker from one of the Magical schools who see matter as the starting point, and spirit as an effect produced by its patterns of interaction. From an overall initiatory point of view this could be helpful; for Magical theory states that such apparently opposing ideas can be resolved at a 'higher level' (this sometimes happens in Science, eg when a wave theory and a particle theory find resolution in a quantum theory). But the temporary loss of 'feel' is definitely a hindrance in a practical working.

So this is one reason why Magical groups prefer to keep their secrets from easy access between each other, and why practical occultists are often very reserved or offhand about their work, whereas those who are voluble on the subject of Magic are generally found to be short of practical experience.

Other people's secrecy is desirable to save you from distraction in a working, but secrecy on your own behalf is also desirable. This is the point where my explanation falters and only experience can help.

There seems to be a link between free communication and leakiness in Magic. Although this is very clear in some theoretical frameworks (eg exposing your plans is a dispersal of 'etheric potential'), it is also an almost universal factor in Magical systems. I cannot think of one where complete lack of secrecy is desirable.

What do I mean by the need for experience? Simply this: practice some regular Magical ritual or meditation beyond the point where you are still under the influence of its novelty, and then study the difference in its effectiveness between: a) a period when you practice on your own in complete secrecy; and b) one when you let everyone know of your practices, what you are doing, when and why. The difference will probably help you to understand the importance of secrecy in Magic.

Of course the idea mentioned in Chapter 7A, that we are living in a self-debugging virtual universe, provides a model for this. Drawing too much conscious attention to paranormal experience evokes the debugging software to normalise it. Surprise is a commodity that does not stretch very far, and that is the tragedy of the media.

Another aspect of secrecy comes in group work. For example, in a system of initiation with several grades (as will be described in the Chapter Nine), it is common for the syllabus of higher grades to be kept secret from those in lower grades. The reason for this is obvious in view of the above remarks: it avoids 'leakiness' and builds up psychic tension. It is also desirable from a psychological point of view: the air of mystery adds strength to the Magical framework of a kind that would only hinder Scientific work.

No further justification for secrecy will be given, because there is no more I can give. But even that confession is helpful in an understanding of the apparently secretive Magician: very often he has no words for what he is doing, only a 'feel' for it. I am doing my best in this essay by the abundant use of inverted commas, but often the links in a Magical chain are so subtle that they are best left out of reach of unsympathetic minds.

YE SEVEN YCLEPT KEYS OF CONCEALED WISDOM ANENT YE MAGICKE ART

1
The journey begins with observation. Note how much normal every-day experience lies beyond the scope of scientific enquiry.

2
Observe then the chaos of the normal and you begin to see its patterns.

3
With the recognition of patterns there grows skill to predict, pre-empt or manipulate phenomena.

4
Some of these results will verge upon the miraculous - these must be met with studied nonchalence.

5
Do not retreat from the miraculous by ever insisting that "there must be an explanation" or that "it must be coincidence". Nor be dazzled by the miraculous - avoid above all the temptation to tell the world what you can do.

6
Transcending the miraculous, you evolve towards pure celebration of "that which is".

7
By this path of Magic you will have crossed the divide between Science and Art, and far more surely than those who would describe the journey in terms of "madness", "delusion" or "folly".

CHAPTER 8A
Yar boo sucks

Experienced and initiated Magicians will, of course, recognise one vital omission from that brief discussion of Magical secrecy.

I refer, of course, to that Great Arcanum whose origins are lost in the Primal Mists of Aeons. That Divine Wisdom of the Ancient Ones passed down by word of mouth by the Chosen Elect. That Hermetically guarded Secret of the Illuminati about which we have sworn upon our blood, our sanity, our very existence to ever hold silence.

One man, Ramsey Dukes, stands boldly in the Highest Temple of the Mysteries. He steps resolutely forward and grasps the curtain to the Inner Sanctum, the Holy of Holies.

Reader! Shade your eyes before they are blasted by that awesome radiance which blinded Paul on the road to Damascus, that Truth which is too much for lesser minds to bear...

Will Ramsey rip apart the curtains?

No.

He will not.

CHAPTER NINE
Progress in Magic

In trying to present a different approach to living, or an alternative way of thought, in elementary terms it is necessary to go back to the barest essentials of the subject. But the danger of revealing just the skeleton of any subject is the danger of revealing a lifeless skeleton.

One's reaction to an account of Magic such as this could be "how very intriguing, but I can't see why people get so excited by it?"

People do get excited by Science, don't they? People have spent years of their life in laboratories, denying hunger, poverty and the advice of well-wishers, in order to make some Scientific discovery. And yet Science has been described in this essay in no less skeletal a form than Magic.

The difference is that we have all some experience of Science, and that experience has given us a feeling of the driving force behind Scientific endeavour, that is to say the sense of progress.

As was mentioned in the Chapter Seven, the theories of Science are progressive, and it is this sense of progress which raises Science from intellectual gymnastics to a way of life. But Magical theories are not progressive in this way, so what can there be in Magic which could make it into a lifelong passion instead of just a funny way of looking at things? This chapter will attempt to answer that question.

If a Magical student attempts some operation to the best of his limited ability and it fails, then it is normal to feel that his Magic has failed. One cannot be expected to meet all the conditions of a complicated Magical working: in this cissy socialist era the tongue of a hanged man can be hard to come by and it may be necessary to make do by strangling a younger brother. But provided the intentions were correct, one still would feel that it was in a sense the Magic which had failed.

In Scientific work the attitude is quite different. If an experimenter runs out of ammonium carbonate and so makes do with ammonium nitrate, then proceeds to drop the test tube, there is no question of suggesting that Science has failed. Probably the experiment will never even be written up, ie as far as Science is concerned, it never took place.

It is tempting to say that this difference in attitude gives Science an advantage over Magic that is 'unfair'. But fairness is irrelevant in this context: all that is revealed is another distinction between Magic and Science.

In Science the theories are imperfect, and are constantly being revised. In Magic, however, they are perfect and untouchable. On the other hand, in Science it is assumed that the operator (ie the Scientist) is perfect whereas in Magic the operator is imperfect and himself in need of improvement.

These assumptions lead to the above difference in attitude in the following way. Because Science assumes a perfect Scientist, it ignores a result which stems from his own defects: as far as Science is concerned, the man ceased temporarily to be a Scientist as he performed the experiment, and so the result is irrelevant (the word 'Scientist' is being used in a stricter sense here than elsewhere). A perfect operator is assumed, and therefore needs no mention: the write-up of an experiment never refers to the absent-mindedness of the laboratory staff, or their tea breaks. But because Magic assumes an imperfect Magician, it accepts and so identifies with his errors: we say that 'the Magic has failed' and perhaps overlook the fact that the Magician is part of that Magic.

Here then is where the real excitement lies in Magic: it is in the possibility of the Magicians being able to work upon themselves and improve themselves according to some chosen scale of values. This can make Magic every bit as compelling and absorbing as is Science with its possibility of working and improving upon our knowledge as expressed in its theories. Indeed, as was mentioned earlier in my theory of cycles, the person who is attracted to Magic in search of power or wordly effectiveness, will usually find themselves gravitating towards a path of self improvement.

The scale of values by which the Magician judges his progress will of course appear as a subjective one to the eyes of a Scientist. It should in fact be based upon some transcendent Spiritual aim, just as the Magic theories should be. It is no good, Magically speaking, to say that your definition of perfect is '£100,000 a year, a pretty wife and two fine children in a house in Hampstead'. A much more satis-factory idea would be that 'perfection means independence from the limitations of circumstances', but even that definition would need to be revised when death draws near.

Given then that there is some subjectively-felt idea of perfection, and of movement in that direction, this aim can permeate and enliven all systems of Magic. Even if your only Magical practice is divination, then you probably begin with the obvious desire to improve your skill. But because the idea of perfection must be transcendent it cannot stop there. With time you realise that the need to practice divination reflects inadequacy upon your part, and so yet greater skill comes with less frequent use. This is very irritating to Scientific friends who demand more proof of your ability as you progress; but the need to impress such friends is itself a limitation which must be overcome.

Although the sense of progress in Magic often exists as a less obvious and conscious compulsion — in which form it is likely to be over-looked by the newcomer to the subject — yet it is seen and under-stood most clearly when it is formalised in a system of Initiation. In systems of Ritual Magic such as Witchcraft, initiation plays a very important and obvious role to the extent that it dominates other work.

For the purposes of devising a system of initiation, you need not only a strong sense of the direction in which you wish to improve, but also a Magical theory around which a system can crystallise. So let us take the theory of the four elements as an example and devise a system of initiation based upon it.

How shall we represent the theory? Let us say that "each human consists of four elements, Earth, Air, Fire and Water, so to perfect the human we must perfect each of the four elements within."

But where do we begin? What do we actually do?

The representation chosen is a good one: it is not one which is likely to prove a limitation, but it is too good to start with. So keep it in mind whilst choosing a temporary representation on a more mate-rial level.

Earth is the flesh or substance of our body, Water is the blood and liquid secretions, Air is our breath and also the air taken in through the skin, and Fire is our energy. So the initiation requires us to gain mastery over, or perfect, each element in turn.

As it stands, however, these four grades add up to a system of Hatha Yoga which would contribute to a healthy body but would not provide much emotional, intellectual or spiritual satisfaction. In fact most people would grow out of this purely physical (Earth) interpretation of the four elements, and realise the need to work also on the emotional needs (Water).

Again we start with Earth: it is no good trying to perfect your emotional nature against a background of ill-health. Water corresponds to the need to achieve harmonious emotional relationships with others. On this level an 'Air' initiation would require skill at communication, and a 'Fire' initiation would involve coming to terms with one's ambitions.

This interpretation too has its limitations, so the whole cycle can be reconsidered on an intellectual or 'Air' level. Perfecting the mind would involve first mastering the body so that thought is not continuously interrupted by its process, and secondly the achievement of emotional stability for the same reason. Thirdly there is pure intellectual exercise in order to clarify thought, and fourthly meditation in order to determine the limitations of thought.

I will not attempt to interpret the model in the Spiritual World.

Thus the original simple four-stage example has extended in a 'wheels within wheels' manner to a system of sixteen grades, each relying on the mastery of the one before it. Such a scale might prove satisfactory to an individual Magician because, although apparently eight grades have to be passed before there is any intellectual stimulus, in fact the very process of devising your own grades and exercises as you proceed means that you are achieving on all levels at each step.

But for a group it is better to provide grades where each step involves some work on several levels in order to encourage the members. Therefore the first, or Earth, grade despite being heavily biased towards the physical would also involve the corresponding ideas on other levels. The idea that the body should be mastered so that it does not impede thought would thus be introduced straight away, and appropriate meditation practices suggested.

For a large group it is also desirable to have a much more formal syllabus. As described so far, every step is just about impossible, ie who can achieve complete mastery of the body in a lifetime, let alone do so as the first of many grades? So in practice earlier grades will be less demanding. If a time is fixed for each grade, it is best to make sure that the span of time includes some complete cycle, preferably a whole year. This is because the problems of working with the element Fire, for example, are different in summer from what they are in midwinter; at noon they are different from what they are at midnight. So a Fire grade which did not involve a whole year of practice would be incomplete. Of course the problems also change from one year to another — eg as we grow old — but that is too much to allow for, so it is best to compromise with one year.

A course of initiatory grades is then set out, a year for Earth, another for Water, another for Air and another for Fire. At each stage there is a lot of set work, but it is also assumed that the candidate will devise his own additional objectives because this ensures that he has a deeper understanding of the significance of his grade.

At each stage work will be done on every level but will be biased towards just one of those levels. For example the third year is the Air grade and will therefore be biased towards the intellect, involving taking classes in mathematics or whatever mental skills are most wanting. But achievement in this grade would also demand skill at every other aspect of the element Air. If you were a poor speaker, you would need to study elocution, and how to clarify your thoughts for debate. Certainly you would be expected to have obtained some proficiency at Yoga breathing exercises — and to have experienced their effect on the thought processes. Similarly it is a good year for long walks in mountain scenery, to see if the air there is as stimulating to you as it has been to great thinkers in the past. You might even join a gliding club — if the relevance of gliding to intellect is obscure to you, then all the more reason for trying it.

Each example that comes to mind seems more and more tenuous in its relevance to an intellectual grade; this is an illustration of the analogy in Chapter Three. During a year of effort and meditation upon the significance of the element Air, a myriad of tiny experiences and achievements falls into place: when autumn comes you notice that certain types of leaves fall directly and others spin and tumble, and you say 'Ah, I see'. But the chances are that what you have just realised is too trivial to explain to anyone else; it is only important to you because it is a small part of a jigsaw which has found its place. Using the previous analogy we have an infinite series of terms $1/2 + 1/4 + 1/8 + ..$ each more trivial than the last and yet all adding up towards a final unity.

Even for a Magician it is not easy to grasp the final unity in these early stages, and thus it is that the year should culminate in a dramatic ritual, to mark and complete the achievement. Of course this ritual should in an obvious way serve as an examination of the skills which are necessary for that grade, but it is much more than that. It is also a hotch potch of what might be called 'mumbo jumbo'. Such a crazy concoction needs to be very carefully devised by people who have a lot of experience and skill in this field because its make-up must involve all that infinitude of trivia which were too small even to have occurred to the aspirant in his year of study and yet which are needed to complete the series. Thus it is that the ritual will contain all the symbolism of the element Air, and quotations from mythology which may not be clearly understood even by those who have devised the ritual. This is a situation where an element of secrecy has its place — exact knowledge of your superior's deficiencies is unhelpful at the early stages! And thus it is that the ritual is not just an exam, but the climax and completion of the year's work.

This also explains the curious use of the word 'initiation' for what might seem to be a process of 'termination'. The year leading up to the Air initiation is seen not as a year spent within the Air grade, but as a year of begging to be admitted to it. The initiation ceremony is the point when the door is opened to you.

The four grades above suggested correspond to the first tour grades of the Hermetic Order of the Golden Dawn which flourished around the end of the nineteenth century. This order set a standard which others have followed, so it is best to study the published version of those rituals and corresponding syllabus for a more complete idea of what is involved. The Golden Dawn initiations run to a total of more than four grades because a larger scheme is used. What is more, it should be noted that later grades grow increasingly less easy to master.

The process of formalising the initiation for group working might seem to defeat its original purpose: why set a time limit of a year when different people might demand different times for different grades? In what sense can one year of intellectual effort be compared with a 'mastery of the intellect'?

The answer is that group working requires a compromise, but that every precaution must be taken in trying to overcome the limitations of that compromise. Already it has been suggested that the formal syllabus should incorporate the student's own ideas for additions to that course. Many systems of initiation demand also that members of each grade have pupils in the grade beneath, and that initiation into the next grade depends upon the successful initiation of your own pupil. This helps to remind you that the achievement of a particular grade does not give you the right to ignore its lessons in the future.

The example of an initiation hierarchy was described at length because it represents Magical progress in its most obvious form, and a form which is of most interest to non-Magicians. Although this formal scale of progress is only encountered in Ritual Magic, a similar idea of increasing attainment is found in all systems.

It is tempting to say that when the idea of progress is absent, then it is not Magic but just the use of a Magical technique. But this is not altogether true. For progress is not always a continuous process: a student who takes up divination may spend a few years finding out about it and picking up the skill, without any conscious idea of self improvement. However he is unlikely to remain in that state for ever, He may simply 'grow out of' divination, or he may actually grow into a more involving system of Magic. Even in the theory of Astrology there is an idea of the twelve signs being a symbol of a man's evolution.

It was suggested that my one example of an initiatory scheme failed to illustrate how diverse were the possibilities for a scheme of progress in Magic. So a very different example is here appended in order to give some idea of the breadth of possibility. This example seems much closer to the idea of Religious mysticism, but there are distinctions upon which I will not elaborate. It starts from the idea that consciousness, and so 'higher worlds', arise from patterns developed in matter (and so is at first glance inverse to the example scheme of Chapter Five where matter is seen as lumpy thinking).

Why is it that memories are so golden, or occasionally so black? When I think back to my childhood, despite the horrors of disillusionment from the Great War, I find a certain glowing quality of life which is lacking nowadays. Even the Second World War now has an aura of 'good times'. Of course I can rationalise: I can remind myself of the bad conditions, of my own uncertainty and immaturity, and realise that in no real sense can the past be considered to be any better than the present. But when I desist, this confusion of facts melts away and once more the past is gently golden,

Which is the lie? Do rose coloured spectacles really distort the vision? The question of course is a Scientist's. What many people forget is the fact that rose tinted glass does not superimpose a colour which does not exist in a scene, but rather it filters out all other elements. So from a rosy point of view it presents what is arguably a clearer picture. As far as we are here concerned, there is no lie.

The Magical theory being suggested is that the process of memory does not so much distort events, but rather stores them in the form of purer essence — after all, whisky keeps better than beer. Any event as experienced is a pattern of interacting cells. In order to preserve it, we distil from it the simple elements of that pattern and relate them to existing patterns in the brain. So when I recall an idle period of my youth spent in Mediterranean bars, although I can rightly argue that I was at the time bored, uncertain and disillusioned, I cannot help a glowing feeling that comes from an association of that memory with such archetypes as 'the Englishman abroad', 'dissipated youth' and no doubt other even more majestic symbols. The Gods are the simplest elements of all experience, pure distinction being the Supreme God, so my past owes its glory to being closer to the Gods.

So what is being suggested is that the greater glory, sense of purpose and beauty that we see in past events is not a lie superimposed by our corrupt brains, but the revelation of elements which were really there and are in fact obscured by the complications of the present. So we seek to improve ourselves by developing the ability to witness the magic of the present as it happens, and not merely when it has become the distant past. What better way to withstand the seductions of nostalgia?

Like all the best Magical ideas, this one goes completely against normal belief: mostly we tend to cherish the complications, inconsistencies and confusions of our mind. We are afraid of simplicity because we feel that a human who had purged himself of this cloud of complications would become cold and 'inhuman'; so much have we identified with complexity. But surely we can only sympathise with one another to the extent that we have some elements in common? So surely anyone who had reduced himself to those simplest elements would, far from being inhuman, be the most truly human and sympathetic of us all? Such a person would pass clearly through all our petty strifes and deficiencies, and go straight to the heart of us all.

It is particularly in China that we find this Taoist-type ideal: the sage who is like the uncarved block from which all other forms can be made. As a system of Magic, it is akin to some of the ideas of Austin Spare. It links with the theory of reincarnation: for it is only when we have simplified our minds to the most basic elements of the pattern that we can expect a conscious reincarnation.

In such a Magical system, initiation stages are replaced by a continuous striving towards simplicity, and yet the progress still is marked by steps: an event disturbs you more than is necessary, you seek to eliminate the implied imbalance, and a whole complex of possibilities is 'mastered'.

Teaching in such a Magical order is less obvious to us: the master must harass the student until he is clear. It is more the way of the Zen master than of the Western schoolmaster.

CHAPTER 9A
The Wisdom of the Great Initiate

Alas, there has been so little progress in my life that, after 30 years, I feel unqualified to add anything to this sublime chapter.

Aha!

Progress in modesty!

CHAPTER 10A
Morality, Magic and Religion

This is a whole spanking new chapter to replace the original Chapter 9 ('The Magical Revival') which has been reconstituted in Chapter 3A.

The original book was written at a time when Magic was high fashion having displaced the materialism of the 50s — and nobody was giving a tinker's cuss for boring old Religion. So the original essay focussed most clearly on the differences between Science and Magic, as that was where confusion was currently strongest.

In the 90s, however, Religion is considered vaguely cool, and people are going on about morality as something which matters rather than something we are eager to transcend. So I add this chapter to address some differences between Magic and Religion, and their different ideas of morality.

LOOK, MUM! NO MORALS!

In a sense the omission of morality in the original text could be justified by saying that morality has no place in Magic. As suggested in Chapter 3A, Magic lies the direction of supreme skepticism, of absolute belief in absolutely nothing, so what place has morality there? I will, however, argue that this lack of morality in fact gives morality especial importance to Magic.

I am, of course, writing about formal systems of morality. These have their origin and home in the Religious sector of our compass. The word of God, or social recognition of 'the Good', tells us of right and wrong. As we progress to the Science sector morality does not vanish, it simply evolves. Just as we progress via monotheism to the Scientific monoreality of physical systems, so also we progress from doing Good in all its forms to one ethical imperative which is to revere Truth.

However, as pointed out in Chapter 1A, the direction of Magic is not towards Good, nor towards Truth, but rather towards Wholeness. A Wholeness in which Bad and Untruth also have their part. So, no matter how wicked or false something is, it should really be acknowledged and dealt with in the Magical sector.

Media moralists and rationalists talk about bad things as being 'unthinkable' — and that very usage sets some of us a challenge to show that everything can be thought. For, although the ultimate arbiters in Magic are Feeling and Observation, nevertheless Thinking and Intuition are also highly respected and should not be insulted by assuming such arbitrary limits to their reach.

As an outright demonstration of 'thinking the unthinkable', let me suggest that Adolph Hitler was not a disaster for humanity but rather a necessary purge to reveal mankind's hidden and denied faults. Let me compound this blasphemy by suggesting that future centuries will recognise him as a second coming of Christ, necessitated by the fact that the first coming failed to redeem mankind because Christ did not sacrifice enough. Jesus only crucified his body and left his integrity, humanity, image and reputation intact, whereas Adolph blew the lot.

Oooh! It's an extraordinary thing to write such words in a book. It gives me a slight shiver, because I know that at least half the world will somehow assume that at some level I must really 'mean' them. I can now be quoted out of context as a Nazi when, in fact, I am every bit as cross about Nazi atrocities as anyone else I know.

Magicians, however, will understand that one can step into any belief system to serve a purpose — which here was to demonstrate Magical freedom to think the unthinkable. I also call to my defence Artists, for they too might understand that, just because Shakespeare wrote that it was sharper than a serpent's tongue to have a thankless child, it does not necessarily mean that he was in any way a stickler for family values.

I can write what the hell I like and you do not know the least thing about me. You don't even know if I wrote it.

MAGIC'S MORAL SENSE

At this point I sense a wave of adoration and love sweeping towards me from the Religious sector. This grateful gift of thanks stems from recognition that I have given strictly Religious people a priceless treasure: namely, confirmation of their darkest suspicions about the evils of Magic. Until this point Magic was beginning to sound horribly nice and reasonable, now they can relax, knowing that it is indeed nothing short of a demonic abomination.

At the same time I feel a wave of unease advancing from the Magical sector — did I not suggest in Chapter 3A that a discussion of morality was the best way to disturb a Magician?

The fact is that most Magicians are, in view of what I have said so far, surprisingly moral people. Indeed, the very fact that moral codes have no place in Magic is the reason why morality plays such an important role.

Remember that I am talking about directions, so when I say that moral codes have no place in Magic I am idealising beyond the horizon. In fact there are moral codes in Magic as practiced. A typical one is Crowley's "do what thou wilt shall be the whole of the law". Though it sounds to a Religious person like a license to do what the hell you like, it is actually an injunction simply to act according to the wholeness of one's being. There is a variation of this used by some Pagans — along the lines of "do what thou wilt and harm no-one". This is a little more cynical (and therefore more Magical?) because it admits the possibility that the wholeness of being might actually intend harm, whereas Crowley's system is limited by a premise that existence is pure joy and so ultimately will work out for the best.

But the real essence of morality in Magic is not such compromises, but rather — as I argue at greater length in my third volume of essays — that when one is stripped of all outer moral codes and injunctions, then you become fertile ground for a discovery of inner moral sense. This is what really happens during the serious pursuit of Magic.

Strict Christians, for example, often claim that, without respect for God and divine law, the world would descend into anarchy, brutality, murder and mayhem. I find it repugnant that anyone should insist that the only thing stopping them from a lifelong killing spree is their faith in a bloke who reputedly got nailed to a couple of planks two thousand years ago. So repugnant, that I call upon the sympathy of Scientists and ask "have not Humanists demonstrated that it is feasible to deny divine law and yet remain impeccable?"

Magicians too are blessed with the discovery that 'anything goes' does not actually force one to do anything. Indeed, it may only be when given such freedom that we come face to face with our own inner integrity.

Instead of moral injunctions, Magical practice demands that we 'clarify' our goals according to those ultimate arbiters Observation and Feeling. It is true that many people enter Magic with pretty selfish or vengeful objectives, but the effort of clarifying them tends to bring us face to face with deeper objectives and so closer to our true wills in the Crowleyan sense.

So, for example, someone who takes up Magic through an addiction to "gimme tunzamunz" will find that this soul-urge needs to be clarified into "I wish to become stinking rich". But is that clear? No, it has no time-qualifier — who wants to become rich on their death-bed? So the urge is further explored and is refined to "I want enough money soon enough to feel that I am a powerful person who deserves respect from society". This in turn could refine to "I wish to feel effective and thus earn respect from society, and I wish for money to help further this aim" But what is the 'effectiveness' one seeks to be directed towards? And so the refining process continues.

Another person might take up Magic with the even more morally ambiguous aim to destroy all racists. This then can refine, through a desire to destroy racism, towards a desire to increase love between all humankind.

As explained in Chapters 3A and Nine, we can enter Magic with pretty crude motives, but the actual practice not only refines these motives but brings us closer to a discovery of a personal inner moral sense which seems to say "precisely because everything is permitted, therefore I discover that I am not only free to, but actually wish to, make choices". And exploration of that sense (which moralists might call 'conscience') leads us to work upon our own natures and thus towards Art.

I recall debating this point with a lady from the bookshop Stuart and Watkins — once a bastion of outright Magic but grown very tame and New Agey. She suggested that they discouraged the heavy Magic literature (like mine) because the people who asked for it were often pretty dubious characters — power hungry, sad dropouts and all that. I admitted that I could sometimes see what she meant, and yet could argue that the bookshop ban was a bit as if the Salvation Army had shut its doors to people who looked too scruffy, the very people who needed it most. It is the very evil image of Magic which offers such healing because it not only reaches parts of me which other systems of thought would deny or despise, but it also makes something of those crude impulses.

Now 'black' Magic is not the only system which offers a place to power-hungry, sad dropouts: they are also welcomed into neo-fascist organisations. But there their impulses appear to become reinforced more than refined. What has gone wrong?

In terms of this essay, a fascist organisation is a Religion where 'good' is identified with one particular race and mindset. It therefore reinforces, whereas Magic tends to refine.

MAGIC OR RELIGION?

As that last example shows, from where I stand fascism and other politics lie towards the Religion quadrant.

Some people would disagree, but as far as I see it politics is directed towards 'The Good' as much as any Religion, but it just happens not to equate it with deity as such. Instead 'The Good' is equated with 'racial purity', 'the revolution', 'the free market', 'equality' or some such abstraction which can appear little different from deity to those less politically motivated.

Because we are talking relative directions and not clear categories, there can be debate about whether politics and other philosophies are Religion, or can become Religion, or not. In fact, there can even be confusion between Religion and Magic — terms which I posit as polar opposites.

Whereas earlier chapters elucidated the differences between Science and Magic more in order to clarify the nature of Magic by comparison, in this section Magic and Religion are compared in order to clarify actual differences which are often misunderstood. This is probably because, as far as today's rationalists are concerned, Magic is just a worse form of the Religion disease.

Let us go back to the very start of this book. The difference lies not so much in the actual practice as in the thinking behind it. Now, many Religious people at some time or another pray for a result — money, children, the healing of a sick friend. As far as I am concerned, that is Magic, not Religion, provided the belief is that such a prayer might bring about the result. Many self-proclaimed religious people do believe that this is so and some scriptures also encourage that belief.

If, on the other hand, the same prayer is said but the underlying belief is more along these lines "Lord, your ways are mysterious so I can do no more than surrender the welfare of my sick brother to your mercy. Nevertheless, as a human being cast in your image it is my nature to wish for help and so I offer this prayer" then I consider the same act of prayer to be Religion and not Magic. It is more about a personal relationship with ultimate good than directly trying to heal a brother.

What then of the Pagan fire festivals? For many modern city pagans these are celebrated in order to restore their contact with the currents of nature — whether deified or not — and so they belong to Magic. In ancient times it was done in order to invoke fertility, and that is certainly Magic. But insofar as it is done as a pure act of celebration, then it is Religion in these terms.

Now this is getting silly — provided that you think I am simply trying to clarify distinctions. Instead, however, unlike the finger pointing at the moon, I am trying to illustrate the pointing process rather than define a strict line between Magic and Religion.

Going back to the previous context, the person who joins a racist organisation because he believes that Jews are 'bad' — and that he is therefore aligning with 'the good' against them — is therefore acting Religiously. If the same action is taken because of a rational calculation that the expatriation of Jews would improve job opportunities for him in the City, then the act could be classed as Scientific. If it was performed because "Dad's a bit of a pacifist wet and I'm pissed off with him and reckon the best way to get up his nose would be to do a bit of nigger-bashing", then the same decision could be an act of Magic. Whereas if he joined the organisation purely because he digs the skinhead style, then it becomes Art.

What I am countering here is the notion that these distinctions have no significance in face of the obscene reality of the act. Knowing the thinking actually helps to inform counter-action. In the case of the Scientific reason, it is probably countered by an analysis of a Jewish role in creating, as much as filling, jobs. In the case of Art it helps to recognise that fashions are ephemeral. In the case of Magic I draw attention back to what was said above — if only he could recognise that it is a Magical act, that rebel has started on a voyage which will lead via other routes up Dad's nose towards a discovery of what he really wants.

That only leaves the most dangerous motivation, which is the Religious one. The very definers of morality have created a moral problem for us.

RELIGION VERSUS MAGIC

As that last shot across the bows suggests, I am championing Magical morality against Religious criticism. Although the true intention of this book is not to advocate one way of thought over another, but rather to illustrate four valid and complementary paths, the argument is bound to favour Magic because it is the most popularly discredited path and thus most in need of reinstatement against its critics.

The basic argument for Magical morality against the Religious is an analogue of the liberal versus disciplinarian debate. The latter demands strict guidelines to keep errant human nature in check, while the former demands freedom to allow the goodness of human nature to reach fruition. The liberal blames human wickedness on the distortions of exaggerated discipline and dogmatism, while the disciplinarian blames it on a lack of moral guidance or standards.

This debate is too well worn to need further comment by me. Instead I will simply illustrate how communication can break down between Religion and Magic on questions of morality, just as it can break down between Science and Magic on questions of fact.

Recently there was a bit of fuss in the papers about a football coach who said that he believed in reincarnation and that, as he saw it, if someone was born with a physical disadvantage in this life it was probably a reflection of past karma.

Now, reincarnation is a theory strongly associated with certain religions, which I believe to be equally useful as a Magical theory. As a Religious theory it stems from an intuitive understanding that the universe must be fair, coupled with a logical explanation of why it can appear to be unfair. As a Magical theory it has more to do with observation that nature is permeated with progress towards wholeness because living things seed the future — so why shouldn't souls make progress too?

From a Magical perspective, then, karma is not about morality but about natural law. So when a reincarnationist ascribes your present affliction to past karma, he is not saying that you did anything 'wrong' in the past. Nearly all the media debate on that football coach began with an assumption that he had blamed physical disability upon 'past sins' — and that this was offensive to cripples. This media version seems highly unlikely, however, because the concept of karma is an alternative to, and not a refinement of, the concept of sin.

Consider, for example, two superb physical specimens — tall, strong, fit and utterly healthy — who both train and become world class athletes. One of them is killed suddenly at the height of his career having never known infirmity, while the other lives on into old age and dies in a wheelchair at 98 years old. Of the two, the first might well incarnate as a cripple, not because he had done anything 'wrong' in exploiting his body in athletics, but simply because he had not experienced the fullness of human existence which includes discovering the limitations of the body in sickness, injury and old age.

I say 'might' incarnate as a cripple, rather than 'will' do so, because this example makes no assumption about what had already been dealt with in previous lives. There is also another possibility: the first athlete, although never knowing physical infirmity directly, might have come across it in a loved one and might have dedicated a lot of time to empathising with the handicapped and assisting with charitable work — in which case there would be less need to balance his next life with physical affliction. This balancing mechanism is so easily interpreted in Religious terms as 'punishment for not thinking of handicapped people' coupled with 'reward for selfless dedication' that it requires a positive effort to see karma as a totally neutral balancing process, with no judgement involved. The media commentators did not make this effort, and they typified a Religious distortion of Magical ideas.

"Handicap blamed on sins of the past" is a double misinterpretation of karma; firstly because it assumes that there is something 'wrong' about being born handicapped, and secondly it deduces that the actions which lead to this 'wrong' state must therefore have been 'bad'. The Magical urge towards wholeness does not classify into right and wrong in this way. I am glad that I was not born with a physical handicap — hardly surprising because I have got used to certain limitations in my life and have no wish to add to them — and yet I also understand that it might have been very good for me. A physical handicap might have reduced my ability to be a jack-of-all-trades and have focussed my intelligence into a narrower channel. I might have become a best selling author and world authority on something instead of a frustrated generalist. So, what did I 'do wrong' to have been handicapped thus with a fit and demanding body?

The purpose of this example is not to demonstrate that Religion sucks, so much as to illustrate how easily communication can fail between Magicians and those with ingrained moral assumptions.

LOSING RELIGION

Chapter 3A suggested that the sort of spiritual and moral authority which Religion has held over the past two thousand years is being lost to Science, even though there is a current movement away from the intellectual authority of Science towards Magical ways of thought. So, once millennial fever has abated, Religion will go onto the back burner for quite a while.

Religious people feel very worried about any decline in Religion, and it is easy to say something glib about human need for Big Daddy God or Mummy Goddess and a fear of growing up. The same can be said about

Religion as politics: the human need to be part of a nation or herd and not stand up as an individual.

Has Magic more to offer than glib criticism?

In Chapter 7A I gave an example of a Magical argument to support a belief in God, an argument designed not to clash too hard with a Scientific education. The argument concluded that the universe was probably a conscious being, in other words, that there was a supreme God of our universe. If Magic can do that, why do we need Religion?

Well, Religion can offer more. For a start, the Christian religion claims that God really cares about each and every one of us, about every sparrow and every hair on our heads — whereas I stopped my argument at a deity which stood in relation to the universe as our mind relates to our body. Do I care about the well-being of every cell and molecule in my body in that personal way? Not really, though as our understanding of cancer grows we might begin to care about every cell, and its creative whims.

This idea that the universe really cares, and that our intentions really matter, is one of the things that people fear to lose when Religion goes. The rise of Science goes along with the loss of a sense that we are all being part of God's plan, instead we have a stronger sense of individual identity.

In Thundersqueak I suggested that a big issues of the coming Age of Aquarius would be those of Leo opposing Aquarius — the individual versus society, kingship versus the herd instinct and so on. In Words Made Flesh I drew two metaphors for the relationship of the individual to society — the 'cog in the machine' and the 'drop in the ocean' — and suggested that we had moved on to the second metaphor now.

The cog in the machine was an older image: in it each of us is like a cog, of no value in itself but a vital part of the machine. This is like feudal society where every person knows their place and has the comfort of knowing where they stand, but little sense of individual identity.

We are now more like drops in an ocean. Unlike a mere cog, the drop of water is as valuable as the ocean itself because it is a microcosm of the whole — all the physics and chemistry of water is contained in that one drop and the ocean is no more than a giant extrapolation from it. But consider that drop as part of the ocean and it is utterly insignificant, it has no justification or sense of importance as the cog in the machine has.

Science has liberated us cogs from the Religious machine and revealed our complexity. We are now shiny drops reflecting the world around us in all our individual glory. But Science, with its acceleration of communication, has also brought us to the ocean. I see myself as a drop — an individual with a vital message to give to the world — but when I try to express it I am brought face to face with the fact that I am one of millions of unwanted writers clogging up the in-trays of thousands of unwanted publishers when all that the

131

world really needs is a steady flow of best sellers from leading celebrities published by a couple of top publishers. The same is true for everyone — hopeful pop stars, bright eyed school leavers, revolutionaries, inventors... we all feel our enormous value as shining drops, but when we approach the ocean we just melt into insignificance. Science has given us a cruelly indifferent universe compared with a God who knows every hair on our heads.

So what can Magic offer as healing? There is nothing to match the fatherly face of God in the 'believe nothing and so believe everything' Magical mentality — but there is the principle of homeopathy.

My original model for this principle was of a family that separated out its trash before leaving it for the dustmen — recyclables in one bag, the rest in another. Then a neighbour puts the 'Scientific' argument that there is no point in wasting time doing that because the council simply puts the whole lot into the one shredder (this was in the early 70s when environmental issues were not taken so seriously). If the family were Magicians they might still go on separating the trash, I argued, because they could choose to believe that such rituals of dedication to the environment can have value in themselves, quite apart from any Scientific causal value. Like a homeopathic transformation, the intention of the individual drop can have a positive effect upon the whole ocean. (The extreme version of this is in alchemical projection, where the perfection of the individual as a tiny seed of philosophers' stone, can transform the whole mass of metal into gold.)

This Magical theory, of the value of individual acts of dedication, is another reason why Magic and Religion can look similar to outsiders. Both Religious and Magical families might be found separating out their trash in the face of council indifference — the Magical family because they believe it can be an effective ritual dedication to Gaia, and the Religious family because they know that, whatever the council does with the trash, God is still aware of their efforts.

So this homeopathic principle does something to restore the sense of helplessness and hopelessness that we can all feel in a inter-networked world of many billion inhabitants.

Even more is offered by the Magical principle of the Universal Mind referred to in Chapter Seven. Taking the virtual reality version of it as example, the idea that we are programs in a vast information process is an idea which can resolve the duality of cog/machine versus drop/ocean. As programs we are like the drop, a microcosm of the whole virtual universe — all the laws of programming lie within us. But insert the program into the larger program and it does not dissolve into insignificance; instead, like the cog in the machine, each sub-routine is also a vital, necessary part of the whole.

Thus we can retain in Magic the liberating notion of individuality inherited from a Scientific revolution, and yet restore that sense of importance within the whole which Religion had once provided.

So cheer up, you Religious bigots — and others!

One further matter. I illustrated the directional nature of my compass by suggesting that Magic, Art, Religion and Science represent movement towards Wholeness, Beauty, Goodness and Truth respectively. This is risky because there are devotees of each who will insist, for example, that "Art is really about Truth", Science is about Beauty or Religion about Wholeness.

On the one hand such apparent perversity simply reflects the fact that these capitalised words represent concepts in what I called the spiritual world where opposites tend to coalesce — so Wholeness, Beauty, Goodness and Truth are really one and the same, corresponding to The Good of Plotinus. At a humbler level however, it reflects a the sort of muddle my compass tries to clarify. So a Scientist appreciating a theory's beauty is simply exercising a human right to persue Art within Science — and this only seems paradoxical, or a diminution of Science, if we forget our directions and imagine that my diagram defines four competing categories. See also Chapter 11A.

"Nothing is true. Everything is permitted"

Those who accept this axiom of chaos magic most fully are those who make the most careful choices. Because they know that - without moral or spiritual absolutes - the self can only be built upon the decisions we make.

CHAPTER ELEVEN
Conclusion

One of the images used by Johnstone to illustrate his different techniques of thought was to compare the so-called 'Unknown' to a swamp. He explained that there are basically four ways to explore a swamp. First, like a hydroplane, you can move so quickly that you do not sink in. Secondly you can fly above the swamp. Thirdly the swamp can be covered over by constructing a solid platform so that an ever-increasing area of it becomes sound dry land. Fourthly you can spread your weight over a greater area so that you can cross the swamp without sinking.

The first technique was analogous to what he called Artistic thought. It could be used to explore far into the Unknown at great speed, but although the traveller came back with exciting tales, he was usually unable to give very precise directions as to how he travelled.

The second technique was compared with Johnstone's 'Religious' thought. It too gave a far reaching view, much more clearly set out, but it was very much of a bird's-eye view and tended to be inferior to the Artistic method in that it lacked real contact with that which was distantly seen.

The third technique was the Scientific one. Scientists were like people in wheelchairs who needed firm level ground to move about. So when they became interested in some distant area which had been described by Art or Religion, they set about extending their concrete platform in the given direction. This is a very slow method; the dry ground gradually extends whilst shady dogmas are cut down and soggy hypotheses filled in. But once the new area is reached, there is a tendency to say 'this bit is as boring as the rest of it — what were those lunatics talking about?' For the very process of exploring has done so much to change what was being explored, hobgoblins and foul fiends having rushed away into the jungle at the sound of the first myth being exploded.

The Magical method is very much one of spreading your weight. It is slower and often less exciting than Religion or Art, but it does enable you to develop a very detailed and close understanding of the areas explored.

In this plan no one technique is considered to be ultimately superior to any other, therefore it would have been nice to have given equal weight to each. Nice but clearly impractical. Firstly my own inclination towards Artistic thought means that I have little to say on that subject. But above all this is an essay on Magic, and that is therefore the most fully explained of the techniques: the others were only mentioned so that contrast could better illustrate the main subject. However the bulk of the comparison has been with Science: this is because it is the most widespread and best understood system of the four. Inevitably, therefore, this essay will seem to some to be an attack on Science, championing Magic in its stead.

Although this is far from being the aim of the essay, it is true that some destructive observations about Scientific method have been made, because no less aggressive an approach is likely to have any impact on those who have been brought up not to question the authority of Science except in jest. Had Religion still been dominant, it would have been necessary to make similar criticisms of that method and so on; for no technique is at its best when all-powerful. What is more, it must be realised that some of the apparent attacks on Science are nothing of the sort in my own eyes, but would seem so to Scientists because of their own form of morality. I ascribe to Scientists a large element of what in their own words would be described as 'self-deception'. This might seem to them a slur, but. as far as I am concerned it is an element which is basic to all consciousness, and therefore I am here admitting the validity of Scientific method rather than denying it.

No system is ultimately superior, but our own limitations are such that we tend to incline more to one system than another, the majority being content with the system they are brought up with. If the reader is quite happy in his acceptance of Scientific authority, then there is no need for me to tell him or her not to bother about this essay. If however the reader feels ill at ease with his education into what seems like a bizarre and artificial way of thought, then perhaps it will be encouraging to realise that there are equally respectable alternatives.

A more tedious way of expressing this is to suggest that there are some of us who fall short of the ideal of the rational materialist; either because of a defective brain structure, or because of defective programming of that structure, their minds are capable of registering experiences which are not only impossible but actually meaningless to a purely rational mind.

Two alternatives are open to such people: either to be treated by surgery, drugs or psychiatry until they become 'normal' or else to come to terms with their own version of the universe. Both have their dangers: in the second case you will be setting out to explore a world which is much less clearly charted, a large and peculiar world where things can happen which could never happen in the rational world. The 'danger' is that you will be seduced by the excitement of this new world, even imagining that the rationalists envy you with your greater freedom. Most people arrange some sort of compromise in practice, but sometimes it is an uneasy compromise and such people would do better to realise the distinction and to embrace it consciously. For the encouragement of such people this essay was written.

Lastly a word for those cabalistically inclined readers who studied the title of this essay in the light of the Notaricon: would you be very disappointed if I failed to expose the Sex Secrets of the Black Magicians?

Ah well, it is quickly done — vide infra.

THE END

CHAPTER 11A
A licence to depart

In this book I have defined four directions which I called Magic, Art, Religion and Science. I then used those terms — keeping the initial capital where appropriate in order to remind the reader that they were mine own terms, defining a *direction* rather than a *region*.

I also needed to remind myself of this, because I surely have at times written about Science and Magic as if they were regions as commonly understood. I cannot help at times using the term 'the North' as a vague catch-all for the region where men start wearing cloth caps, keeping whippets and saying "by gum, yer cheeky munkey", but it does not mean I have forgotten that the term really defines a compass bearing.

Most readers will surely continue to use the words magic, science, religion and art to define regions even after reading this book. That's ok. It is useful to have the terms North, South, East, West used as regions as well as directions, and we can accommodate both uses at once — when the weather forecaster announces that there will be "cold North winds in the East" we understand well enough what is meant. So too can the reader go back to talking about science and magic as different countries, without losing the benefit of being able to refer to my compass when necessary.

As an example of one individual view of religion, I quote from a paper called *New Science New Religion New World* which is an expansion of a talk given to Woodbridge Quaker Study Centre, Birmingham, September 1998, by Frank Parkinson. He writes:

"... I should state in advance that I consider genuine religion to have three characteristics: it is a systematic attempt to know more about the nature of a hypothesized creating power, to establish an appropriate relationship with it and to take steps towards self transformation."

In my terms, Frank Parkinson is here defining a region of human activity which he calls "genuine religion" and I, as a Magical thinker, am quite happy that he should define that region in his own way. As an explorer of his region, however, I take out my compass and say that it contains three sub-regions. What he describes as "a systematic attempt to know more about the nature of a hypothesized creative power" I would describe as the Science of his region — even though I recognise that it might not share any territory with the region which Richard Dawkins describes as "science". His wish to "establish an appropriate relationship with it" is what I would consider to be the Religious quarter of his religion, and his "steps towards self transformation" are what I would indicate as the Magical quarter of his religion.

It is tempting to try to reshape his definition by paring away the Science and Magic bits and say "the only really Religious bit was the second bit". To support this I could quote his later remark "The end of religious evolution, from the present standpoint, is to establish a relationship with the primal power...". However, any attempt to say he is 'wrong' and that I can subdivide his religion and 'purify' the concept would be a mistake, because it would mean I was beginning to accept my four directions as four sub-regions, and so slipping away from the proper Magical use of my compass as an aid to navigation.

Instead of thus reducing his definition, let me attempt a more positive exploration. Surely, we should be able to discover a fourth region in his religion — an Artistic region? A fourth characteristic of genuine religion which could be described as 'celebrating the hypothesized creating power' or 'expressing the feelings engendered by the relationship formed with it'. Why has Frank Parkinson not included this region? I note that he is also a poet — so maybe he simply took it for granted.

Whereas the critical use of my compass which tended to break down and diminish the region he called 'genuine religion' could be seen as an act of aggression, I like to think that Parkinson would welcome my second use of the compass, and thank me for reminding him of that fourth part of his genuine religion.

If I turn back to Richard Dawkins, who must also have a personal understanding of a region which he calls 'science' and which lies within a region which may be called 'rational human activity'. I assume this is so, because he clearly wishes to defend this region from irrational tendencies which lie beyond its borders.

I have already used my compass within this region of his, when I pointed out in Chapter 3A that his desire to change the public perception of science was in fact a desire to do Magic, in my terms. It is a Magical spell to banish Magic, and that some people mock his endeavours because they more or less unconsciously recognise this irrational element in his work. I also pointed out that, by fostering the notion that ideas can evolve like life forms and occupy territory in the ecology of human culture, he had evoked the demon that New Age Magical ideas might be proving fitter to survive than his own ideas.

Again, there is a temptation to use this compass to attack his work, breaking it down and saying that bits of it are 'not Scientific'. instead I would like to salute him and offer the discovery that even in his polemic approach I can find Magic, Art and Religion as well as Science. The talk he gave at Cheltenham about 'unweaving the rainbow' held genuine poetry for me, as well as being good Magic. He is a also a great preacher... Hi there, Richard!

So I conclude by allowing a return to the normal use of the words art, science, magic and religion. It's only human, and one book won't break the habit of ages. Like a true amoral Magician, I accept that with a shrug. My theory is being given the license to depart. In the first edition this was done more dramatically, in a chapter which has been re-written and put earlier in this edition. So I will now append the closing words to the original Chapter 9.

In view of this, it is clearly desirable that there should be an effort to divert the cycle from its obvious course, and to encourage mankind to be honest and admit to Magic. For only when we face up to Magic and recognise it as such can we hope to learn to control or come to terms with it. Until that time it is a dangerous quicksand beneath a paper-thin floor of bogus Scientific jargon.

With this in mind, Lemuel Johnstone initiated a Magical operation to alter the course of human destiny choosing the time of its commencement as a moment which, expressed in years, is equal to the fourth power of 6.66, ie the number of the Beast extended in three dimensions of space and one of time. The final link of the operation was begun at a time which, expressed in years, equals 1974. 9136 or the square of 44.44. This moment of time, Cabalistically considered, so symbolises the principle of growth of plans that it can

be considered as the instant of equilibrium before commencement
where the least effort of conscious will could suffice to alter the entire
destiny of this planet

The climax of this operation's working can be expected at a time
equal to the four dimensional extension of the number 6. 66666 when
..

(Has he gone mad? Isn't it a pity to spoil a sensible essay on Magic
with all this Armageddon nonsense?)

To many readers, this whole chapter would seem a blot on my thesis,
for it is only in this chapter that there has been a major departure
from cosy theory into historic fact. Why has this essay been mined by
a clumsy and ill-researched attempt to extend its ideas into the field
of history and of prediction? If I really wanted to impress, why didn't
I back up my vague pronouncements with some accurate dates and
quotations from reliable sources?

It would have been perfectly possible; a number of relevant
volumes are at hand. A Scientist can produce historical evidence in
support of his theories by carefully selecting those examples which fit
his hypothesis, and rejecting those which do not as being insuffi-
ciently well-documented — for otherwise the reason for their not
fitting his theory would be apparent in the documentary evidence. In
just the same way a Magician can support his ideas by selecting the
facts which feel right, correctly considering other facts to be merely
an obscuring influence, This is no fraud; this is simply the process
upon which our consciousness, and therefore our universe, is founded
— the Religious arguer rejects deceitful facts, the Artist rejects whatever he or his aesthetic chooses.

Why then was my argument not better supported? Why make a
fool of myself?

It could be argued that there is a paradox in Johnstone's thesis in
that it could never be put into a form which might convince a
Scientist without disproving one of the basic deductions of the thesis
itself. I therefore defend myself from the embarrassment of 'recognition' by playing the fool.

However this argument merely obscured a more Magical purpose:

this theory of Johnstone's is being given 'the license to depart'. It has served its purpose; it has proved helpful in an era which led up to the writing of this essay. During that time it began to amass evidence, and even proved that it had predictive ability. In other words: Johnstone's teaching-aid was getting too strong a hold on our lives, and was beginning to exert an influence upon the universe. So it gets the license to depart; it is dismissed.

Prediction is the Waterloo of any philosopher: the prophet of doom offers himself as a voluntary sacrifice which is sufficient to postpone the doom he prophesies. For the announcement of a doom is the stimulus which leads the world to take steps to avoid that very doom and thus cause the prophecy to fail. Thus the reputation of the prophet is slaughtered. But of course a prophet's reputation is everything, so it is the prophet who dies. Only Artists can survive prophecy — for no-one recognises their prophecies until after they have been realised.

A Religious prophet exposes himself to ridicule, but knows that the true faithful will stand by him. Recently there has been a torrent of Scientific prophets, not one of them successful, and so far the press shows no sign of tiring of them. When a Magician makes a prophecy, he similarly exposes himself to ridicule, but his consolation is that he does it with a better understanding of what is involved.

I ridicule my theory in this last chapter in order to dispose of it. I ridicule it to save myself from any danger of 'acceptance': but there are still likely to be people who only read on in order to find out just how much of my argument is spoof, just how much I really believe, just how much can be proved. Here is your last lesson: I will not tell you, and even if I did you would do well not to believe me.

Too slavish an acceptance of Religious and now Scientific authority has led us all to depend too much upon others for our ideas of truth. One expert makes an interesting observation, and we are glued to our television in order not to miss other experts' views of his opinions. A book presenting a sensational new version of evolution appears and becomes a bestseller: instead of accepting or rejecting it in the light of our own experience, we wait for other books to be written which either support or attack the first one.

There was of course the temptation to dress up Johnstone's ideas in pseudo-Scientific jargon, including a wealth of quotations, references, a bibliography, a ton of 'evidence' and a title such as "Man: The Irrational Animal". That's just the sort of treatment that gullible publishers love, and the script might have been accepted by a reputable publishing house and been professionally and properly edited , but Magically speaking it would have been an appalling piece of self- deception to fall for such temptation.

If the favoured Scientific image is that of the cool and rational observer, then the favoured Magical image is that of the wandering Fool. Only when laughing is the Magician safe from pride. The uncertain student begs me to give some definite signs by which he can tell if a possible Magical Teacher is a fraud or not, but I can give no such signs. For the ultimate decision is yours alone, and a good teacher will force you into such a position that you have no other defence but your own judgement. It is often said that a true teacher never asks for money: but I assure you that a true teacher would start to demand an extortionate fee if he suspected that you had no other tests of his worth.

So many people approach Magic with the wrong ideas that a Magical teacher soon realises that the best way to dispose of pupils who are cramped by experience is for the teacher himself to arrange to be caught cheating, for those who are cramped by morality the teacher had best appear immoral, for those who are cramped by ideas of greatness the teacher should appear feeble and ineffectual, and so on. The few pupils who survive these hurdles are either geniuses or idiots; both are adequate.

So you must forget your authorities and observe. Make up your own mind how much of this essay is true, how much of it is a clumsy attempt to say something which is true, how much is fraud and how much is error.

Appendix A
Bibliography

1. Books from The Mouse That Spins

Johnstone's Twentieth Century Occult Philosopher And Skepticall Politick Theorist. 1971

This was my first effort, inspired by a prediction by the palmist Mir Bashir that I would become a writer addressing a small but educated readership but that it would never be my first source of income. Sigh. How right. It is a sort of novel, an ouevre de jeunesse, that I might one day publish out of a sense of completeness. It might alternatively make a curious film.

Uncle Ramsey's Bumper Book Of Magick Spells. 1972

Really just an addendum to the previous book — essays by the individual characters. It will only be published if I put it together with other early essays as Volume One of the collected essays.

SSOTBME An Essay On Magic. 1974 onwards.

This is the book you are now holding.

Thundersqueak — The Confession Of a Right Wing Anarchist. By Angerford and Lea. 1978 onwards

This was a complementary book to SSOTBME dealing with the dark or obscurer issues.

Words Made Flesh. By Ramsey Dukes. 1987

A fuller exploration of Johnstone's concept of an information universe.

Blast Your Way To Megabuck$ With My SECRET Sex-Power Formula — and other reflections upon the spiritual path. By Ramsey Dukes. 1993

Volume 2 of the collected essays published in collaboration with Revelations 23 press.

What I Did In My Holidays. By Ramsey Dukes. 1998

Volume 3 of the Collected Essays, published in collaboration with Mandrake of Oxford.

The Good, The Bad, The Funny — De Arcano Nostrae Sanctissimae Mirabilisque Trinitatis, Eius Potestate Sanandi Et Redimendi Vim

Statistis — Ad Quae Excoginatio Eius Contributionis Ultimae Ad Magisterium Magicae Artis Nostrae Addita Est. By Adamai Philotunus

An exploration of trinitarian, as opposed to dualistic, thinking written in 1993 and first published in paperback in 2002.

The Hellgate Chronicles. By The Hon. Hugo C St J l'Estrange.

The collected edition of The Satanist's Diary which ran from the late 70s to early 90s primarily in Arrow.

Slo Joanz — Kali Yuga.

A sci-fi novel which may one day emerge from the mousehole.

2. Other works referred to

The Laws Of Form. George Spencer Brown. Details unknown, as I must've lent someone my copy.

Unweaving the Rainbow. Richard Dawkins. Details unknown, as I have not seen it but only heard him talk about it.

The Origins of Alchemy In Graeco-Roman Egypt. Jack Linsay. Details unknown, as I cannot be bothered to get up and look. I can see that it has a silver cover from where I'm sitting.

Towards A Magical Technology. Tom Graves. Details unknown, because I cannot now find it on my shelves.

Shadows Of Mind. Roger Penrose. Details unknown, because it would be a bit unfair on the other books if I only gave details of this one.

Appendix B
The New Age and Magic

In Chapter 2 I look at specific areas of Magic and in Chapter 2A I add some examples to bring the book more up to date. One Magical area which has emerged since this book was written — and some say because the book was written — is the 'New Age'. I am covering the New Age in an appendix because it is a rather special case.

Anyone acquainted with New Age ideas will see that they definitely fall within the sector I have described as Magic — the emphasis on feeling over logic, the subjectivity, the solipsism and the personal growth are all factors shared by Magic and the New Age.

But the New Age is more than just a specific technique or set of ideas, indeed it is a movement as broad as Magic itself. So do we consider Magic and the New Age to be one and the same thing?

On the one hand they have so much in common at the theoretical level, on the other there is a very different atmosphere about the two, to the extent that they can appear to their respective devotees as near opposites or rivals. Some New Agers see Magic as irredeemably sinister, just as some Magicians see the New Age as pathetically wet. And yet the people I classify as Scientists would dismiss both groups as cranks — with Magic being counted a particularly dotty subset of the general New Age delusion rather than being a great embracing sector of human endeavour.

This paradox is not dissimilar to the often violent antipathy between Catholics and Protestants — a distinction in which the two groups can perceive themselves as utter polar opposites, while those not involved could hardly tell the two Religious groups apart.

Although it could be hard to define a clear distinction between Magic and the New Age, I believe that differences are beginning to emerge.

On Saturday I was in the biggest bookshop in Cheltenham with a friend and I glanced at the Magic section in the spirit of market research. I found three bays under the heading "Mind Body and Spirit" which I have come to recognise as a euphemism for New Age. I noted that "Science" only occupied a single bay. Under MBS there were sub-heading for Astrology, UFOs, Myths, Paganism, Witchcraft and so on... but there was none for Magic. This was a new development — so I scanned the other sections to see where the Magic books had been allocated, and I found none.

This was disturbing for someone currently engaged in publishing books on Magic. So I asked an American literary agent who visited me that week-end about current attitudes and she confirmed that the word Magic is now considered to be a negative marketing proposition, and that she even had an author who was currently reframing Magic into more acceptable terms for today's publishers.

That night I wept. For all my life I have been continuing Crowley's work of explaining Magic in as clear and undogmatic manner as I could, hoping to dispel superstitious fear and invoke understanding and sympathy and delight. To his Magick Without Tears and his Magick In Theory And practice I had added mine own elementary textbooks like this one, and now the bookshops had closed ranks with the publishers to exclude my babies.

Three bays of New Age books and not a single Magic volume — so at least the marketing folks recognise a clear distinction between Magic and the New Age.

Mine own views on this distinction have been spelled out in an essay in What I Did In My Holidays, so I will only review them briefly here. They quote Crowley's concept of three aeons which bear no relation to the cycles of history suggested in this book (Chapter 3A). According to Crowley a new cultural impulse is beginning this century on a par with the cultural change symbolised by the birth of christianity. I argued that the position of the New Age in this transformation might, in retrospect, seem analogous to the position of Pauline christianity in the previous era.

As I saw it, Christ's teaching invoked ideas of tolerance, love and forgiveness which were highly revolutionary in terms of the dogmatic and inflexible assumptions of the pre-christian era. This christian message proved too radical for its time and it might not have survived had not St Paul repackaged it in a less tolerant and more dogmatic form which people found easier to swallow. On the one hand you could argue that St Paul corrupted Christ's message, on the other you could say that christianity only survived because he knew how to market its core values — and these include a vision of perfection through the imitation of Christ.

So I considered the possibility that the New Age was a similar exercise for today. It amounted to a rephrasing of the core values of Crowley's thelemic philosophy, whilst retaining the concept of perfection which really had no place in thelemic relativism.

Rephrasing this in the terms used in this book, I would say that the New Age is very much the same as Magic as described in these pages, except that it has been modified by restricting the wholism which I believe to be fundamental to Magic.

What Religious people fear about Magic is that it embraces Evil as well as Good — as I explain in Chapter 10A it is not advocating Evil but simply more prepared to recognise its place within creation. What Scientific people despise about Magic is that it embraces Falsehood and Illusion as well as Truth — with the same qualification as before. (Art people are more tolerant, but they do reserve the odd sneer for the cheesiness of Magical symbol-ism.) The New Age salves those fears by accentuating the positive and elim-inating the negative so all is discussed in terms of "light" with little reference to the role of darkness except as an error waiting for the light.

The result is a version of Magic which is not intimidating to the public — "Magic Without Fears" in place of Crowley's "Magick Without Tears".

Now I really love the New Age, and I reckon it does a superb job at promoting the positives and giving a great deal to humanity. I love it because I still have Magic to handle my negatives. But I am myself anxious about the possibilities of a New Age without Magic — as in those bookshop shelves. As explained at length in my other book, such religious devotion to the Good, or Light, or Purity, or Perfection without some balancing attention to the negatives could lead us down the path beaten by the Nazis if we are not careful.

So I was unhappy about the lack of Magic on those bookshelves. And I was disappointed in the way things seemed to be going. The publishers, like the media, have turned their backs on Magic. Whereas New Age books are reviewed with derision in the more serious press, books on Magical theory and practice get no mention at all. They do not seem to understand that, by allocating a position for Magic beneath their contempt, these people's contempt for the New Age amounts to a form of recognition — reflected now by three bays of shelves to Science's one.

I would not expect Scientists to champion Magic, but they might at least recognise that it could prove a more lively opponent. Magic might offend Science by seeing it as an 'alternative world view', but that is at least a neutral assessment compared with the judgmental New Age concept of an 'outdated patriarchal paradigm'. Magic could at least offer a vigorous sparring partner for rationality, whereas the New Age would simply absorb and overwhelm it.

Simply because the New Age presents itself as an easier target for mock-ery by the rational mind, thus it has been fostered like a cuckoo in the Scientific nest while Magic has been pushed aside.

So here is our final test for Magic. An author weeping in the early hours of the morning at his failure, because booksellers have joined the rest of the business world in believing that the branding is more important than the product. What is he to do?

He should recognise that the idea that "the branding is more important than the product" is itself a Magical principle of such profundity to almost amount to a definition of Magic itself. He should allow the world to make its choices as he has made his own. He should consider whether life might not have intended more for him than simply to be a conduit for philosophies. He should recognise that the end of writing will free great reserves of enthu-siasm for other pursuits.

But will he?

This book now has three successive endings — just as it has three successive beginnings. The sort of indulgence only enjoyed by those who publish for themselves. Amen.

THE GOOD THE BAD THE FUNNY

DE ARCANO NOSTRAE SANCTISSIMAE MIRABILISQUE
TRINITATIS, EIUS POTESTATE SANANDI ET REDIMENDI VIM
STATISTIS - AD QUAE EXCOGINATIO EIUS CONTRIBUTIONIS
ULTIMAE AD MAGISTERIUM MAGICAE ARTIS NOSTRAE
ADDITA EST

by

Adamai Philotunus
(Ramsey Dukes)

Polarised, dualistic thinking is the driving force behind intoler-
ance, prejudice, domestic strife, social turmoil and world
conflict. People have long understood this and have long
pleaded for unity - either as a return to a previous oneness, or
as an advance towards a higher synthesis.

In doing so, they have simply taken sides in a new polarity -
Unity/Duality.

This book suggests an alternative, a genuine solution. It asks
what would happen if we thought in threes as naturally as we
think in twos? If, in place of a God/Devil duality we were
brought up with a God/Devil/Trickster trinity?

This solution is explored in depth - as a philosophy, as a
psychology, and as a practical way to heal the divisions in society and in our selves.

This is a course in practical mind-alchemy, with suggestions for
further work. It also proposes an entire revolutionary magical
system based on a trinitarian instead of the traditional fourfold
model - plus a full account of Ramsey Dukes' infamous
"Cybermass of Thrice Greatest Data-Hermes".

**285 pages with five chymical plates by Louise Hodson plus over
60 diagrams in text.**

Paperback edition ISBN 0-904311-10-4 available now from
bookshops or from www.occultebooks.com

MORE FROM THE MOUSEHOLE

BLAST
your way to megabuck$
with my *SECRET*
sex-power formula...
..and other reflections upon the spiritual path

Volume Two of the collected essays of Ramsey Dukes

He appears more than ever a combination of Robert Anton Wilson and Tommy Cooper... The
Peter Pan of the British occult scene, and long may he go on diverting us.
Paul Geheimnis, Chaos International No 15

For an unbeatable title see 'Blast Your Way to Megabuck$ With My SECRET Sex Power Formula'
- thoughts on masculism, magic and the metaworld from Ramsey Dukes. Virtual Gonzo.
David Profumo, Daily Telegraph Books Of The Year, November '93

Something of Arthur Koestler, something of Loa Tzu, a pinch of Kant and a dash of Genghis Kahn
- Ramsay Dukes is magnificent... Humourous, witty, written with flair and economy of style, this is
certainly one of the most thought provoking and genuinely radical books I've read in a long while.
If you are hacked off with old ideas and yearn for new vistas, you could do a lot worse than let
Ramsey Dukes be your guide.
Julian Vayne, Pagan Voice Autumn '93

☞Why does there seem to be less magic in the modern world? *Could
it be because we are all better magicians?*

☞ Is it time to reinstate the Charlatan in his vital role as initiator on
the occult path?

☞ Is scientific thought declining in favour of magical thought, and is
this inevitable?

☞ Have men traditionally played a leading roles because of a deep
sense of their own uselessness relative to women? *And is this situation beginning to reverse?*

☞ Might we not be living with another's virtual reality? *How would
this effect our understanding of this universe?*

These and other questions are explored in depth in this volume that
brings together essays written in the 1980s by one of the most original and creative contemporary writers on magic. Available now as e-
book from www.occultebooks.com, paperback due Summer 2003

Open your mind to a breath of fresh air from Ramsey Dukes

What I did in my holidays
Essays on Black Magic, Satanism, Devil Worship and other niceties

Volume Three of the collected essays of Ramsey Dukes

Is it ok for a national government to negotiate with terrorists?
Should we be prepared to make a pact with the demon Terrorism
– or should we remain forever sworn to the demon No Compromise?

This is a book about demonolatry.

It was never meant to be: it began as a cobbling together of all the essays and stuff written in the last seven years. But it turned out to have a pretty consistent theme.

A theme that begins with Crowley's "Aeon of Horus" and the new, Thelemic morality. From that viewpoint demonic pacts are reappraised: are they not a negotiation with the demonic, as opposed to sworn allegiance?

Many old and new demons lurk on these pages: black magic, sexism, elitism, satanism, publishers, prejudice, suicide, liberalism, violence, slime, bitterness, old age, war and the New Age.

These demons hold keys to power and wisdom.

They are prepared to negotiate.

Are you?

ISBN 1-869928-520
First edition, 1998, published in collaboration with The Mouse That
Spins (TMTS) by: Mandrake of Oxford.
410pp Felstead 80gsm paper, stitch bound.
Available from all decent bookshops.

THUNDERSQUEAK

or the confession of a right wing anarchist - being the
suicide writings of Liz Angerford and Ambrose Lea

"As well as being a particularly fine introduction to the practical
side of the occult, Thundersqueak could almost be regarded as one
of the ur-texts of Kaos, if not the one that set the kaos-sphere
rolling." - *Head Magazine, issue 5*

"Thundersqueak is definitely on my list of Top Ten Most
Influential Books That I Have Read" *Rodney Orpheus*

"This is a book to turn you on to so many things; it's hard to
know where to start.... I suppose at a pinch this could be called a self-help
book- as there are instructions inside that you can follow, and by doing so
make your life better (or at least more interesting)- and perhaps happier-
even if "the only true happiness is to live dangerously in times of peace, and
to be at peace in times of crisis" ... but New- Age fluffy it is NOT! This is
'self-help by self psychic-surgery': It tears your self to bits and chucks out
the crap." *Kate Hoolu on www.occultebooks.com*

"A WITCH IS A REBEL IN PHYSICS AND A REBEL IS A
WITCH IN POLITICS"
Thomas Vaughan, Anthoposophia Theomagica, 1650

"A KING MY CHOOSE HIS GARMENT AS HE WILL:
THERE IS NO CERTAIN TEST"
Aleister Crowley, The Book of the Law, 1904

"BRUTALLY SHALL I TEACH THE GOSPEL OF SOUL
SUICIDE"
Austin Spare, The Anathema of Zos, 1924

Paperback edition, facsimile of first edition, available now from
bookshops or from www.occultebooks.com